THE MODERN PRESIDENCY

St. Martin's Series

in American Politics

———

Stephen K. Bailey   THE NEW CONGRESS

Allan P. Sindler   POLITICAL PARTIES IN THE UNITED STATES

David G. Smith   THE CONVENTION AND THE CONSTITUTION

THE
MODERN
PRESIDENCY

Grant McConnell

UNIVERSITY OF CHICAGO

ST. MARTIN'S PRESS · NEW YORK

Contents

I MYTH AND SYMBOL   1

    Constitutional Powers
    The Work of the Presidents
    Symbol and Substance

II THE PEOPLE'S CHOICE   16

    Constitutional Provision for Election
    The Uses of Parties
    Primaries and Conventions
    Campaigning
    The Achievement

III PRESIDENT AND CONGRESS   34

    A Shifting Relationship
    The Intricacies of Government's Concerns
    Presidential Legislation
    Legislative Party Organization
    Special Interests and Groups
    Measures of Presidential Success

IV PRESIDENT AND EXECUTIVE   52

    The Executive Machinery
    Bureaucratic Responsibility
    The Executive Office
    The Bureau of the Budget
    The Autonomy of Federal Agencies

V PRESIDENTIAL LEADERSHIP   69

    The Prestige of the President

Mobilizing His Support
Decisions and Alternatives
The Character of the President

VI THE PRESIDENCY IN THE POLITICAL ORDER   86

Federalism and the Presidency
The Fragmented Authority

The Presidents   99

The Constitution on the Presidency   101

Bibliography   106

Index   110

THE MODERN PRESIDENCY

Chapter I

MYTH AND SYMBOL

Thirty minutes after the shooting of John Fitzgerald Kennedy, thirty-fifth President of the United States, two out of every three adult Americans knew of the event. Within another hour nine out of ten knew.

Attempts to explain the profound outpouring of emotion in the days and nights following were halting and often contradictory. Yet the funeral was hardly over before the making of a myth began. It was not the first occasion in American history in which a President had become in death and memory more than he had been in life and office. The death of Lincoln was the parallel that leaped to every mind. When Franklin D. Roosevelt died it shook the nation and saddened its people as had few other events of his turbulent era. Abraham Lincoln and Franklin Roosevelt were both wartime Presidents and among the great men of history; but similar waves of emotion appeared with the deaths of William McKinley and Warren G. Harding, neither a crisis President and neither of heroic stature.

The presidency is the highest office in the land. Yet the office is not a given quantity and never a known factor in any political equation. Its character varies with the character, activities and views of the man who is President. Perhaps this quality was nowhere better put than in a statement of Woodrow Wilson before he became President, "The President is at liberty both in law and conscience to be as big a man as he can." Yet it is not true that the presidency is a developing office in any strictly cumulative sense; one President may greatly enlarge it during his tenure, but his successor has no assurance of being able to exercise the newly added powers. The most that may be said is that here is an office of great latency; the presidency is what the Presidents have made of it.

It is also true that to a great degree the President is what the office makes of him. George Washington was well known to the framers of the Constitution. This foreknowledge, however, is exceptional. It would have been difficult to anticipate what sort of Presidents Franklin Roosevelt and Harry Truman would become at the moment each stood on the threshold of the office.

For all that the presidency is a very real office, with space, desks, staff and all the paraphernalia of office, it is ultimately elusive and almost insubstantial. There is a paradox here, since it is by now a cliché that the American presidency is the most powerful office in the world. Although the statement may well be true, it has been so frequently repeated that a vast illusion has been established as to the reach and degree of that power. Amaury de Riencourt, a rather unfriendly observer, stated a few years ago, "We must see in the President of the United States not merely the Chief Executive of one of the Western democracies, but one already endowed with powers of truly Caesarian magnitude." Just a few years after this theory of the American Caesars was announced, a venture in Caesarism was indeed attempted at Cuba's Bay of Pigs; it failed to the point of absurdity. A bit later, it is true, the same President faced down the nuclear might of Russia and forced Khrushchev to order the hasty withdrawal of the missiles installed in Cuba. Here was irony on a colossal scale: President Kennedy could bend the Soviet Union to his will and humiliate its leader, but he could not carry through an operation against a small underdeveloped island republic to the extent of removing its dictator. Ultimately, of course, the success against Russia was largely the failure of Khrushchev, who was guilty of almost insane folly in attempting what he did under conditions of a nuclear stalemate. Both great powers were limited and their leaders narrowly circumscribed by the limits of what either could successfully undertake.

There is a very widespread confusion between substance and manner—or "style," as it was fashionable to term it in the Kennedy era. President Kennedy's manner was forceful and masterful. His office, and indeed the entire executive branch of government, gave the appearance of unity and furious activity. Theodore Roosevelt had an even more vigorous manner and through his very well publicized adventures in the wild west and on San Juan Hill established a reputation of activism which frightened many. By some tests, however, the immediate successors of these two Presidents, Lyndon Johnson and William Howard Taft, had better claims to effectiveness and achievement. Johnson was vastly more successful in completed legislation than Kennedy, and Taft was much stronger a foe of the trusts than Roosevelt. While the appearance of power is sometimes mistaken for the substance of power, appearance is sometimes a useful substitute for reality, indeed it may even become reality. For the most part, however, style is a deceptive index of actual power.

Constitutional Powers

At the moment of American independence, executive power was the form of power most feared and hated by the rebelling colonists. The longest part of the Declaration of Independence was a list of grievances against the king. Yet within little more than a decade the ex-revolutionaries had established a strong executive power, which in time was to call forth the judgment of Henry Jones Ford that here was a revival of "the oldest political institution of the race, the elective kingship."

Experience under the Articles of Confederation was disillusioning to the few but intellectually distinguished and influential men who took it on themselves to frame a new instrument of government. The Revolutionary War had been fought without any genuine executive, or indeed any genuine central government other than Congress, which was itself little more than an assembly of ambassadors from the states. The war had often gone poorly as these ambassadors failed to persuade their sovereigns to meet the financial and other obligations they had undertaken. The army sometimes went unpaid and occasionally the troops melted away under the eyes of their supposed commander. But the war had been won, and perhaps it was reasonable to suppose that such a haphazard arrangement would do for the less rigorous conditions of peace. As each subsequent war has, however, the Revolutionary War gave a definition of goals and a discipline that disappeared with peace. Peace in some ways was a sterner test of government. The impulse to unity and cooperation was gone, and the absence of an institution capable of governing a nation growing in diversity was alarming.

Though federalism and the separation of powers are distinct principles in the American political system, the two were related to a common problem—how to achieve a minimal unity among the factions that made up the bravely announced union. Some of the most powerful factions adhered to the pre-existing units of the states. To alter the state's power was to change factional power; yet a nation could not be created without attaching power-holders to it rather than to the separate states. Federalism was the particular compromise by which this seemingly impossible problem was partially solved. At the same time an institutionalization of the union effected among the states and the many factions was imperative. Congress could not serve in this manner, for its vices were precisely those in need of moderation. The presidency was the means chosen and its deliberate counterbalancing in the separation of powers was the compromise by which the political union became possible.

Among the many decisions reached by the men who met in Philadelphia in 1776 none was more fateful than the formulation of the presidency as a single executive chosen independently of the legislature. A plural executive chosen by Congress, as urged in the New Jersey plan, would have made the adoption of the new constitution easier and more certain. It would have greatly mitigated the conflict between executive and legislative that has vexed so much of American history. It would not, however, have erased the underlying problem confronting the building of a nation; it would instead have tipped the scales toward division and disunion. Such an executive could hardly have avoided representing the centrifugal tendencies which have persisted throughout the years of American nationhood.

The decision, finally, for a single executive appeared in the Constitution simply and directly: Article II said, "The executive power shall be vested in a President of the United States of America." It did not provide for a share in this power by the Vice President nor for a council attached to the President's office (an idea advanced in various forms at Philadelphia to diminish the monarchic aspect of the office). A primary quality of the executive, as Hamilton argued forcefully in *The Federalist,* must be unity. At the same time a compromise had been provided, not only in the formal separation of powers, but in the many checks and balances scattered through the document.

It is difficult to escape a sense that the framers of the Constitution took a considerable pride in their handiwork with the presidency. They had solved a very difficult problem in practical politics, and had, moreover, founded their solution on what was in their eyes the most solid kind of political theory. The practical compromise itself embodied the ideal of balanced government, which the best thinking of the time admired.

Considering the care and skill that shaped the Constitution as a whole and the provisions on the presidency in particular, however, Article II, the part devoted to the office is astonishingly brief—almost, one says, incomplete. The first section of this article is the longest and deals principally with the eligibility and choice of the President. It touches on his compensation and states the oath of office; it creates the vice presidency, but characteristically leaves much ambiguous about this office. Section 2 carries a list of presidential powers; the President shall be commander-in-chief of the armed forces. He may require the written opinions of the heads of unspecified executive departments; he may grant reprieves and pardons. He may with the advice and consent of the Senate make treaties; he may appoint ambassadors, public ministers, consuls, and judges of the Supreme Court, again by and with the advice and consent of the Senate; he may fill vacancies during Senate recesses. He is required to inform Congress of the state of the nation and recommend measures; he may convene both houses, adjourn them when they disagree on a time of adjournment; he must receive ambassadors and other public ministers; he must commission all officers of the U.S.; and must take care that the laws be faithfully executed. The last section of the Article provides for removal from office on impeachment and conviction of the President, Vice President and all civil officers of the United States. Article I sets forth the presidential signature or veto of bills passed by Congress.

Whether taken as a mandate of power or as a description of the office, Article II, and the few supplementary passages elsewhere in the Constitution, are grossly inadequate. The list of functions and duties assigned the President is at once short and sketchy; at points it is vague and trivial. To read it without reference to subsequent history is to discover more questions than answers. Just what process in treaty making is contemplated? What does appointments "by and with the advice and consent of the Senate" mean? Why should space be taken to empower the President to require the opinion in writing of the principal officer in each executive department? What are the executive departments? Are their principal officers otherwise directly responsible to Congress? Why should it be necessary to require him to report on the state of the union to Congress? Does the oath of office confer any power on the President he would not otherwise have? What is implied by the statement that "he shall take care that the laws be faithfully executed?" It might appear to be a general mandate to manage the government, but it is only a fragment of a sentence and is so placed that it is capped by the specific requirement that he shall commission all the officers of the United States.

Neither in whole nor in part do the provisions on the presidency offer great satisfaction about the nature of the office. What is clear—the power to give pardons and reprieves, for example—is minor. What is significant—the opening sentence of Article II and the "take care that the laws be faithfully executed" clause—is cryptic. Even the meaning of the commander-in-chief clause is ambiguous. The relationship between President and Congress is implied rather than stated, and even the implication is understandable only in light of the well-known adherence of the framers to the doctrine of the separation of powers. The greater clarity of Article I on the powers of Congress might suggest that the power of the President could come only from congressional enactment. And yet, if this were so, why should the few items of power given the President in Article II be stated at all? It is difficult to avoid the conclusion that either the framers were extraordinarily careless with this part of their work, or that they had little vision of what they were creating. The former is too harsh a judgment and the latter is more probable.

The conditions of government, like those of life itself, in eighteenth century America were vastly different from those the presidency has had to serve since. In a design intended to endure far into the future, as the constitution was, freedom from rigidity, even toleration of vagueness, were virtues. Only the most essential features could be specified, and even with these, there could be no certainty that things would evolve as planned. The mark of the framers' success with the presidency was that the essentials were incorporated in the office, and they have endured: a single executive, chosen independently of Congress, whose power is limited. It would be impossible to point to any single passage which lays down this last and most important characteristic, but it was everywhere implicit and has persisted down to the present.

The Work of the Presidents

For the rest, the presidency is the work of the Presidents. They have not, indeed, been free to do with the office whatever they have wished or thought desirable for the nation. Congress has persistently taken a different view of the office than the Presidents and has been often able to frustrate presidential plans and hopes. The Supreme Court on occasion has limited the office. The federal structure of the nation as expressed in Congress and in other less obvious ways has severely curtailed its possibilities. And the American people have set barriers to White House ambitions. Within all these limitations, however, the Presidents have been able to create the presidency as we know it today, the most majestic political office of modern times.

Its history has been a continuing dialogue among the Presidents over whether it is endowed with some inner sources of power or not. This is the debate between the "weak" and the "strong" conceptions of the office. Although the differences between these views have been great, they have never been polar: even the proponents of the "strong" position have recognized the existence of limits, and the "weak" Presidents have sometimes acted without reference to specific authorization in the Constitution or in legislation.

The point that was perhaps the single essential of the office was made by George Washington: that the President could and must act at times on his own authority—and that there is such authority. Implicit throughout Washington's presidency, it came out most clearly in the area of policy where challenge was most difficult, foreign affairs. When war recommenced between France and England in 1793, Washington was determined to remain apart from the conflict. The young government accordingly issued a proclamation of neutrality (although the word "neutrality" was not used in view of the divergent sympathies toward the combatants within Washington's cabinet). Controversy immediately broke out over the constitutional propriety of this step. Hamilton, supporting the presidential action, pointed to the opening statement of Article II that the executive power is vested in the President

and to the "take care" clause. Regarding the few specific powers enu-
merated as the President's, treaty making, receiving ambassadors and so
on, no limitation to these alone was implied. The only limitation to
Presidential exercise of *executive power*, accordingly, Hamilton held,
were those expressed in the Constitution.

Hamilton's conclusion that the proclamation was within the President's power leaped past the question of whether the action was executive in nature. Madison, speaking for the opposition led by Jefferson,
caught the gap of reasoning and denied the assumption that such action
was executive. Hamilton and Washington nevertheless won the day.
The real difficulty that the Madisonian argument encountered over
time was that the distinction between executive and legislative power
was less clear and definitive than Madison or Jefferson (or, indeed,
Hamilton) assumed. Washington's act, following Hamilton's argument,
helped establish the more basic principle that there were reserves of
power in the presidency and that these must be used by the Presidents.
The formal constitutional argument was serious, but it was a reflection
of the large dispute between two general visions of the presidency. The
practice of Washington did much to reduce this dispute to one of definition of the boundaries of presidential power: from his time forward,
whatever the formal arguments might be, the President was neither a
figurehead nor an automaton applying legislative and constitutional
prescriptions.

Jefferson's position was something of a paradox. He had opposed
Washington's neutrality proclamation on the ground that it did not fall
within executive power. When the presidency fell to Jefferson then, it
was reasonable to suppose that it would become very different and
more limited. John Marshall, however, made an acute prediction that,
Edward S. Corwin pointed out, proved fundamentally correct: Jefferson would enhance his power as President but weaken the office. As a
party manager, Jefferson demonstrated the possibility of manipulating
Congress, particularly the House of Representatives. Relying on this
basis of power, he was able to act vigorously, but his personal talent
was not readily deeded to his successors. Both Madison and Monroe
accordingly yielded up to Congress much of what the presidency had
meant so far.

This lapse in the character of the office ended abruptly with the
election of Andrew Jackson. There is an almost inescapable tendency to
read history retrospectively and for this reason the popular nature of

Jackson's administration has sometimes been exaggerated. A broadening of the suffrage had been under way, but it was not as dramatic as it has sometimes seemed. Jackson's men, moreover, were not as different from their predecessors or so committed to the spoils system as they have sometimes been represented. Nevertheless, Jackson did understand popular appeals and he made them. Here, probably, was his particular gift to the office: he demonstrated what was inherent in the presidency but obscured in previous thinking about it, that the President is a popular figure. He is popular because he commands the attention and often the imagination of the multitude; as a result he has wide and frequent opportunities to enhance his power. He is also popular in that he is less beholden than Congress to particular fragments of the nation simply by virtue of the vast scope of his constituency. The peculiar history of the American struggle for independence had marked monarchy as unpopular; when the cry of monarchy was raised against Andrew Jackson by Clay, Webster, and others, however, its lack of force was apparent.

Jackson is variously said to have restored, remade the presidency, or to have been the first real President. He has been acclaimed as the first incumbent of the office who stood for the interests and desires of the mass of the people. The issues of his time, however, were different from those which have later invoked class interpretations and in which Presidents have stood as popular figures. The Jacksonian era was turbulent and the disputes still raging about its conflicts are probably too easily seen in sharper terms than the muddied issues of his time justify. Certainly there is a striking paradox about Jackson himself: he favored states' rights but insisted on the autonomy of his own power as President against the pretensions of Congress, the focus of divisiveness. He was willing to recognize congressional power to interpret the Constitution but insisted on his own power as President to interpret the document and to act on that interpretation. The outcome, as with his determined assault which culminated in the destruction of the Bank of the United States, was the establishment of the presidential capacity for *action*. His effective insistence that the members of his administration were responsible to him and not directly to Congress was as important as his sheer activism. This issue of the path of responsibility by administration members was not settled by Jackson—it is still lively today—but Jackson's fire and fury did more than anything else to influence the trend of things.

The position of Lincoln and the measure of his impact on the presidency are difficult problems in assessing the office. More than any President after Washington, he assumed the role of national leader. More than any President before or after, he brushed aside the limitations supposedly inherent in the office. The statements that he was a dictator miss the mark, but his actions at several points clearly crossed the bounds of legality. He has had no imitators in these actions and it is unlikely there will be any. Yet, his influence has to be accounted one of the most important in the entire history of the presidency.

His specific contribution in constitutional terms was to invoke the "commander-in-chief" clause and create from it the "war power" of the President. Certainly it is hard to believe the framers had any inkling when they accepted the clause that it could be used as Lincoln used it. Equally, however, it is unthinkable that the framers could imagine the ramifications of modern war of which the Civil War was the prototype. The "war power," however, has remained vague and ill-defined down to the present. Although it has been invoked in both World Wars, its users have been uneasy about it and have sought to bolster it with references to legislation. Indeed, Lincoln seems at first to have relied almost casually upon congressional ratification of his actions after he had acted, as for example in his wartime advance of public funds without apparent congressional authority.

Despite his virtual creation of this ambiguous, and probably dangerous, constitutional doctrine, Lincoln's importance lay in the intangible and elusive central quality of the office, leadership. Lincoln was a poor administrator despite his choice of very able cabinet members. He sometimes seemed hesitant and self-doubting; he was bitterly hated in his time; he is the one President against whom the charge of dictatorship has any substance. Yet he was the greatest national leader to defend the Constitution more than any other President. His legacy is an office that in crisis rises as the embodiment of the nation and a tragedy-touched myth that will color the presidency as long as the office endures.

As it did after Jackson and after Jefferson, the presidency contracted after Lincoln. The crisis past and Lincoln gone, Congress reasserted itself. Distinguished students of public affairs held the presidency in such low esteem that a foreigner, Lord Bryce, discussed "Why great men are not chosen Presidents." A brilliant young American scholar named Woodrow Wilson titled his examination of the American system *Congressional Government,* indicating his strongly stated thesis. This book, Wilson's first, was written very near the presidency's nadir, at a time of cynicism toward public affairs. But the very changes which made government and the presidency almost insignificant in time produced its own reaction. Farmers' and workingmen's movements signaled the discontent beneath the surface. Gradually the public temper changed and a movement for reform took shape.

Concurrently, the renewal of the office came about, though gradually and the work of no single President. Theodore Roosevelt's flamboyant style once more placed the presidency in center stage, and the re-ascendance had begun. Princeton's Woodrow Wilson rather belatedly reassessed the presidency and in 1907 deplored that some Presidents, "more theorists than statesmen," had failed to use the full power they might legitimately have used. He concluded that the President's "is the vital place of action in the system." It is not altogether clear whether this good academic's dislike of theorists applied to the President then in office. Certainly Theodore Roosevelt had a definite view of the presidency and he was explicit about it. Some years later he insisted, while he was President (or so he claimed), on "the theory that the executive power was limited only by specific restrictions and prohibitions appearing in the Constitution or imposed by the Congress under its constitutional powers. My view was that every executive officer, and above all every executive officer in high position, was a steward of the people bound actively and affirmatively to do all he could for the people, . . . I declined to adopt the view that what was imperatively necessary for the Nation could not be done by the President unless he could find some specific authorization to do it. My belief was that it was not only his right but his duty to do anything that the needs of the Nation demanded unless such action was forbidden by the Constitution or by the laws."

This categorical, and theoretical, assertion was matched a few years later by Roosevelt's successor, William Howard Taft: "The true view of the Executive function is, as I conceive it, that the President can exercise no power which cannot be fairly and reasonably traced to some specific grant of power or justly implied and included within such express grant as proper and necessary to its exercise. Such specific grant must be either in the Federal Constitution or in an act of Congress passed in pursuance thereof. There is no undefined residuum of power which he can exercise because it seems to him to be in the public interest. . . ."

The dispute was highly academic, however, since at the time each theorist wrote he was out of office. It fell to the ex-professor, Woodrow Wilson, to demonstrate the kind of presidency he wrote about. It was most certainly a strong one; its strength, however, derived largely from the war that prevailed through most of his term in office. When the United States entered the hostilities, the "war power" discovered by Lincoln served as a mantle for much of the industrial mobilization without which the war could not have been won. In this sense the presidency was a source of legitimacy to the war effort. It could hardly be otherwise with such vast and novel government activities. Ironically, however, Wilson discovered the boundaries of presidential power in the area in which it would have seemed to be most extensive, foreign relations. His ultimate failure was in the collapse of his design for the peace and the League of Nations.

With the defeat and death of Wilson, the presidency once more lapsed into the near desuetude which had overtaken it after the strong Presidents of the past. Herbert Hoover might have become a strong President after the manner of Lincoln or Jackson, but he was restrained by traits of personality, diffidence perhaps, and a commitment to methods giving vetoes to every group that had reason to oppose specific actions, a commitment dating, curiously, from his experience as an administrator in Wilson's time.

The modern model of a strong President has been Franklin D. Roosevelt. Few Presidents have been so denounced for the vigorous exercise of presidential power as he. His opponents claimed that he arrogated entirely new sources of power; even some of his supporters believed that this was true. In actuality, however, Roosevelt did no more than follow the examples of his predecessors, and did not resort to the extremes that Lincoln had followed. Most of his program rested on congressional authorization, and where he acted without it, he relied upon his undoubted authority in foreign affairs. He cited the "war power," but for the most part buttressed it by congressional authority as well. Less formally, Roosevelt relied upon the resources of party, an area in which he had incomparable skill. However, he also discovered in the group organizations so heavily deferred to by Hoover a source of support Hoover probably never envisaged. In the radio Roosevelt had a tool hitherto unavailable or unexploited. The important thing, nevertheless, was that Roosevelt saw his role as that of leader in a way equaled probably only by Lincoln and by Jackson.

The successors of Franklin Roosevelt have all been in his shadow—as much in power and style as in issues and policy. Harry S. Truman came out of the Senate and might have been expected to hold a more exalted view of Congress than his predecessor. The vision of the presidency as it came from FDR persisted, however, and in his initiative with the Marshall Plan and his dismissal of General MacArthur, Truman demonstrated that he had a firm understanding of the realities of power in the presidency.

President Eisenhower represented the reaction to Franklin Roosevelt and, to a lesser degree, Truman; in this he was as much a captive of the Roosevelt myth as the others. He affirmed a view of the office as limited as Taft's; at times he seemed to believe that the American government system simply required Congress to make the decisions and the President to carry them out. At critical moments, however, his actions belied his statements. In foreign affairs, as in his decision not to intervene in Indochina, and in domestic affairs, as at Little Rock, he demonstrated that the presidency could not be a weak office. Neither John Kennedy nor Lyndon Johnson exhibited any doubt as to the nature of the presidency; in their hands it has been unambiguously a position of leadership to be used to the fullest extent. Yet each has followed Franklin Roosevelt in relying heavily on congressional approval. On the essential issue, however, both agreed that initiative in the American system lies with the President.

Perhaps it is premature to say that the curiously recurrent cycle of "strong" Presidents followed by "weak" Presidents has run its course and that henceforth the office will always be strong. The administration of Eisenhower is not long past, and measuring by modern standards, it was weak. Moreover, no President since Lincoln has attempted to circumvent Congress in his search for authority; the differences have been solely in the determination and capacity to cajole, coerce, and manipulate the legislators. Nevertheless, a large change has taken place in the character of the office. Strength and vigor are now the traits associated with its occupant and, probably, sought by the American people. These are the qualities most conspicuously appropriate to times of crisis. But crisis in the modern era is seemingly chronic. Only for comparatively short periods since 1929 have there been opportunities to relax the sense of urgency that has been the modern lot; only in one of these, the Eisenhower era, has the nation indulged the theory of passive leadership in its highest office.

Undoubtedly, relatively "weak" Presidents will hold the office again. It is unlikely, however, that any will be as restrictive as Taft or as unassertive as Eisenhower. A new set of specifications for the office has gradually evolved out of the years of crisis and the practice of modern Presidents. These specifications can change again, but it will be difficult to make them demand less strength than those that now prevail.

Symbol and Substance

What Harold Laski said of the presidency almost a generation ago is even truer today: it is "the keystone of the American political arch." Yet the office remains almost impossible to define in any but the most superficial terms. Its powers can almost never be stated with certainty or precision. Their description in the Constitution is vague, disorderly, and misleading. They have expanded and they have contracted. They have been interpreted in ways so radically different as to seem to be about different offices. It would almost appear that the presidency is an open mandate for anything its occupant might choose to do with it; and foreign observers have variously predicted doom from it and copied it as a means for imposing tyrannies in their own lands.

But the dangers of the presidency have hardly ever derived from an excess of power in the office; they have often come from its uncertainty, sometimes from its patent inadequacy. An elemental fact of the American presidency is that its powers are limited. The limits change with circumstances and are seldom precisely knowable in advance; they are no less real, however. To some degree they derive from the requirement of legislative authority for presidential action in most areas of policy. The different constituencies of Presidents and congressmen and the array of checks and balances insure differences between the two branches. Yet this array of mechanical checks is by itself not necessarily a sufficient guarantee of limited presidential power. A President lucky in congressional elections and skilled in the labyrinthine ways of legislative manipulation (Lyndon Johnson in his first years in the White House) can do much to circumvent such checks. Increasingly, moreover, a great part of the work of government is "administrative" in nature and so complex that in effect it is beyond the reach of Congress except sporadically. The real limits on the power of the President come from the whole ethos of American government. In part this is to say that a President can wield only the power the American people wish him to. Yet no transitory passion of a momentary majority would be sufficient to give authority for unusual action by a chief executive. No President would be likely to misunderstand it, or, if he did, repudiation would be swift and paralyzing.

The genuine problem confronting a President and American government as a whole is to generate sufficient power for presidential action to match the needs of the nation. To do this a President must mobilize the support of his own constituency—no less than the nation itself. The nation, however, is always something of an abstraction, a diverse, inchoate multitude of men spread across a vast expanse of land. To mobilize these men is to give shape, to organize, to create and recreate the nation. This process is inevitably touched with mystery. Yet here is the essential dimension of the presidency. The greatest Presidents have all ranked high on this scale, whatever their skills as administrators or legislative managers. All have made themselves national symbols; in so doing they have given substance and purpose to the nation itself.

Chapter II

THE PEOPLE'S CHOICE

A President performs one of his most important services before he ever reaches office. This service consists very simply of campaigning. He shares this service with his opponent and, indeed, with all the would-be candidates who have been eliminated in the long tortuous process of national choice; for the process of selecting a President is sometimes itself as important a feature of the office as the emergence of a particular man as President. The contest—and all the conferring, caucusing, bargaining, and scheming—are the indispensable means by which each four years the record of the past is reviewed and a new assessment of the state of the nation is made by the people themselves. Here is the way old compromises are examined and perhaps revised and new ones made among the many elements of the population. It is the occasion on which everyone in one degree or another is called upon to think of himself as an American.

The process serving these awesome functions in the United States is without counterpart anywhere else on earth. Indeed, whether the functions themselves are equally served elsewhere is questionable. Yet the process is noisy, disorderly, contentious, and absurd. The gap between the indignity of the process and the grandeur of the end is enormous. Most foreign observers regard the system as vulgar and ridiculous; most Americans look upon it as a form of circus, but they cannot withdraw their attention from it. The system was never intended as it exists and it is inconceivable that it ever could have been planned.

This paradox is a direct product of the democracy served by the process. The garish vulgarity that persists throughout the electoral campaign reflects the participation of the great multitude of the American people in the political life of the nation. The noise and the contention and the crudities might be avoided if the campaign involved only the genteel and the well-bred. The price, however, would be enormous. To exclude part of the American people is contrary to the ethos of democracy, and its consequences, though impossible to predict, would be dangerous.

Whatever the deficiencies of style characterizing presidential elections and their attendant rituals, the impressive fact is that the process largely achieves its ends. When the tumult has reached its climax on election eve, the issues confronting the nation have been put to debate —if not always in the highest intellectual manner or by the candidates themselves, at least in the press and on the air. At this moment few citizens have not reflected about national policies and how their own lives have been affected. Whether by contact, computer, or osmosis, the candidates have acquired a sense of the land and the mood of its people. Subtly or crudely, they have changed their appeals and their programs to reflect that mood to the best of their abilities.

The objective ostensibly is no more than to win a numerical majority of the votes cast on election day. More than this is involved, however. No election is ever a simple reflection of the preference of the people for one man (or one party) instead of the other; it is a composite register of the desires, frustrations, and aspirations of millions of individuals on an almost limitless number of matters. Some of these topics are concrete, some are general, and some are so deeply emotional they are beyond rational discussion. A presidential election is also a measure of intensity, for not all of those entitled to vote do so; those who feel most strongly on matters touched by politics are the most likely to appear at the polls. The election also reflects elements of power other than sheer numbers of voters, for money and organization play their part in the mobilizing of votes. These may be imperfections by the democratic ideal; they are nevertheless elements of power in the daily life of the nation. Ignored, they may well prove sources of later disorder.

So it is that in the great calm of election day the vote is cast and a decision emerges. But it is far more than a decision; it is the summation of an incalculable multitude of decisions, all of them simplified and compressed into the choice between two men. Should not the outcome be violent? For a whole season the charges, the innuendoes, the promises, and the words have been compounding until the mass would seem to have become critical and explosion certain. In a few breathless hours, however, the tallies are made and the results are known. But long before the results are official the loser goes before virtually the entirety of the nation watching television; with every last bit of manliness he can summon he gives his last great service to the nation in accepting the outcome. And the people, including as a simple matter of course all those in opposition, take the result as settled for another four years.

It is a monumental achievement. The choice of leaders has all too often culminated in civic dissension, defection of the defeated, and disorder. Many modern nations have yet to solve the problem of peaceful succession. An orderly change of leaders, moreover, is a rough index of success in the elementary function of politics, maintaining peace and order among the citizens. That the outcome of elections is taken for granted in the United States is a measure of American political success. On the one occasion of utter political failure, the Civil War, an election was the precipitating cause.

Accommodation and peace and harmony, however, are the minimum ends of politics; they are rarely sufficient. Virtually every political society confronts problems for which governmental power is essential. A stalemate of political forces within the nation might produce domestic peace, but it would rarely allow the solution of these other problems. Herein lies a great dilemma of modern politics. The American political system has been rather less successful in providing its government with the capacity to meet objective problems than in gaining the acquiescence of the people in the government and its leaders. Presidential elections, in turn, have been less to blame for this shortcoming than the manner of choosing Congress and the sheer diversity of the nation. Nevertheless, a President who has been through the experience of a bitter campaign and a close election will inescapably be aware of the narrow limits within which he can safely act. The presidency of John F. Kennedy demonstrated this to a strong degree.

Constitutional Provision for Election

The problem of the power to govern was probably uppermost in the minds of the framers of the Constitution as they formulated their plan for selecting a President. The new Constitution was intended to establish a government capable of action. The presidency was central to the new conception and accordingly by the method of choice they devised they intended to insure that only a man of high standing and competence would reach the presidency. Their constitutional plan, however, deferred to the states and their legislatures, and thereby related the nation's highest office to the principle of federalism directly and not merely through the President's relation with Congress. Election was to be indirect and to operate through the colleges of electors chosen as each state legislature might direct. The legislatures found many ways to pick the wise men who should serve as electors, but for the most part during the brief period the planned system actually operated the electors were the legislators themselves. The system was baroque in several ways and provided a dense filter for the impulses of democracy.

The original plan ran into early difficulty when in 1800 Jefferson and Burr emerged with tied votes; the states then passed the Twelfth Amendment requiring electors to indicate which of their choices were for President and which for Vice President. Already, however, the original conception was on its way to obsolescence. The electors were required by the Constitution to meet in their various states and were thus precluded from acting as a single deliberative body. More important, the franchise was rapidly expanding and other forms of political participation were not to be denied the masses of the people. The party system took discretion out of the hands of the "electors," who became mere registrants of the popular choice. It was democratization in spite of the Constitution.

The constitutional provisions on presidential elections have, nevertheless, had some important effects. A President is still required to be a citizen, a resident, and at least thirty-five years old. The electoral ballots are counted by states and go as state units, the winner of even the narrowest majority in a state taking all that state's electoral votes; the possibility thus remains that electoral votes may decide an election contrary to the indication of a simple count of popular votes. There is even the chance of an elector voting against the wishes of the party on whose ticket he was chosen; this has happened, but not in critical situations. Perhaps more important than either of these possibilities is that under present provisions no candidate may win a majority of electoral votes and the decision may be thrown to the House of Representatives. Minority factions have thus been tempted to run candidates independently of the Republican and Democratic parties in the hope of getting to maneuver in the House of Representatives and so to extract concessions otherwise unobtainable. Such a result is unlikely but a President could accede to office with a serious minority in popular votes and deeply clouded by suspicion. The most important constitutional provision, however, is that the President receive a majority of the electoral votes. This requirement has been one of the strongest forces making for a two party system.

The Uses of Parties

The party system is the essential part of the electoral process as it operates today and as it has since the rise of parties first disrupted the finely laid plans of the Constitution's framers. The parties have substituted an entirely different method which no one ever planned or even foresaw. The constitutional convention was marked by strong fear of the evils mass participation in politics might bring, a fear seemingly justified by the disorders preceding the calling of the convention. As the rise of parties relegated the electoral college to insignificance, the parties themselves provided the organizing principle by which the not-to-be-denied masses could take part in politics in an orderly and meaningful way.

Clearly the party system has not met the tests of statesmanlike discussion and consistent wisdom sought by the rationalist bias of the framers; nevertheless, it has allowed both the broad participation and the scope for accommodation which the pragmatism of the American people has demanded. The appearance of parties effected perhaps the largest single change in the constitutional scheme. It has replaced the question, who will govern most wisely? with, who will govern most acceptably? The second question may be less inspiring; in a democracy, however, it is more urgent. A President however wise in his substantive decisions who failed to carry the people with him would have failed completely.

This substitution of a seemingly meaner question and a lower style of politics for that originally planned for the nation has distressed many Americans. This ambivalence about the political order extends to all the activities of parties and politicians; the very word "politics" has come to refer to party politics only—and is a term of reprobation. The catalogue of sins ascribed to the normal activities of parties is long: the parties engage in endless arguments; they have no principles; they are alike; their leaders engage in cynical bargaining; they are corrupt; and so on *ad infinitum*. These charges have a considerable degree of truth: the parties *are* contentious; they are pragmatic and ready to criticize their opponents; their daily life is filled with bargaining and occasionally there are signs of corruption.

Nevertheless, the distress and contempt are misplaced. Without the arguments and the adversary stance of parties public issues would have far less discussion and decisions on them would often be less acceptable to the American people. And that the major parties have similarities means each is seeking to win a majority of the voters. An election is a competition between attempts to fashion a compromise of all the issues which concern the voters, one that will appeal to the greatest number. Although they will sometimes differ, the compromises will frequently be similar. It indicates similar responses to the same problem and to be similar is not the same as to be unprincipled. Beyond this, the parties do evolve different solutions and they do differ on some important matters. If the differences were as great as some of the cynics appear to wish, the nation would be in serious danger of open conflict and the parties would have failed in their ultimate mission of adjusting differences and preserving the social union.

The larger functions just mentioned are by-products of the process and are not the day-to-day conscious intent of the parties. The specific function of any party is to attempt to elect its candidates to office. To winnow the potential candidates, they must weigh a complex array of considerations. Statements on issues and policy—the platforms—that emerge are part of the large process of political compromise, but they are more immediately directed to the goal of winning office. Where these platforms and policy statements are bland, temporizing, and even vague, probably they deal with matters on which the electorate is itself divided.

Not all elections serve the large and grand functions indicated here, however. In some local elections, the candidates are obscure and the issues of policy may be so undiscussed that they are hidden entirely. Such elections are usually marked by an absence of party competition or even participation. The candidates who thus emerge on the ballot seem to arrive there by something not much better than chance and the whole affair takes on the character of a lottery. Able men may reach office this way, but it is unlikely, and the candidates who succeed do without benefit of the debate and controversy that best indicates the temper of those who must be governed.

Presidential elections are never of this character. The importance and drama of the office make these elections major events and insure that they are always contested. They reinforce the drive for party organization and competition between parties. Their influence extends to elections for offices that in nonpresidential years get little interest and gives them attention they ought to have regularly. A curious paradox lies here. The American party system is organized along federal lines, as laid out by the constitutional order. It has accordingly become a cliché that the parties are more local than national. Yet the parties often show more vigor and substance nationally than locally. Part of the explanation is that American parties are weaker and less well organized than is generally assumed. In many areas of the country they scarcely exist, and in some states—California and Wisconsin, for example—they are heavily inhibited by laws that seek to deny them significant roles. The contest over the presidency often provides what impulse there is for party organization and competition. Without the presidency as a major focus the American party system would probably be vastly weaker than it is.

Between presidential election years, national party organization dwindles almost to nothing. Some continuing party organization persists in Congress, but a visit to the national headquarters of either major party reveals only a small establishment engaged in little activity and without any sense of urgency. If we compare it to any of the strong interest group organizations, it is insignificant. In some localities, it is true, party organization continues active, particularly if other elections must be faced there. But public participation in local party organizations is minor, and often unwanted.

When a presidential election approaches, however, the national organization comes to life. It rents lavish office space, which is pervaded by a great bustle of activity. Locally, the party machines spring into similar activity and their emissaries seek out segments of the public they have not seen since the previous presidential election. Where there is no local party organization other than the nominal body consisting of a few office holders—and this is not uncommon—machinery is hurriedly improvised to reach all those individuals who collectively are sovereign but who otherwise are voiceless.

Improvised and defective as it is, this machinery must find the candidate and get him elected. The first task is at least as important as the second. At the outset the men who would like to become President and have some kind of qualification seem innumerable. Probably most, however, are unknown to the public nationally. Without machinery for their exposure and examination the election would be little more than a lottery. The results might occasionally be good, but there is no reason why they should be. The parties provide both a rough set of rules and the tests that candidates must pass. These tests have a greater rationality than is sometimes evident. Usually a candidate who hopes to succeed must have national standing and high party rank. There have been exceptions; certainly Warren Harding was not a national figure and Dwight Eisenhower had no known party affiliation until just before he was nominated. Generally, though, to be an effective President, personal prestige and party experience are essential.

A serious candidate who hopes to meet the tests imposed by the parties is thus usually a governor of a major northern state or a prominent senator. Again, this rule has not invariably been followed—Wendell Willkie was a corporation executive, Eisenhower a general—but the highest political honor is reserved by the politicians for politicians. This is not merely the selfishness of a particular guild; it is also insurance that the candidate commands the trust of great numbers of his countrymen and knows the ways of the political order through which he must act. Of all the posts that most nearly approach the presidency in the substance of their responsibility, governor and senator are closest. Like the presidency, they demand sensitivity to the needs and aspirations of large numbers of citizens. While the work of governor is exclusively domestic, a senator's involves foreign affairs, and if there is reason for the recent preference of the senatorial route to presidential candidacy, perhaps it lies here.

Even after the field of candidates has been reduced by these first rules of practical eligibility, the list is too long for anything but a meaningless mélée without further winnowing. The conventions that meet to make the final choices have little time, and much elimination must occur before they meet. The manner in which this is done certainly meets no ideal test, but the job does get done. Some of the process is informal and out of sight: the meetings among politicians that evaluate potential candidates in the years between elections. But the most important part comes in the trial period of approximately nine months before the general elections. This is when the candidates try to make themselves known and their ambitions discreetly but clearly understood. In this period they face up to the ordeal of the primaries or find good reasons for not doing so.

Primaries and Conventions

There is a kind of system in the primaries, but it is a curious and disorderly one. Less than half the states have presidential primaries, and these are northern or western states influenced by the doctrines of Progressivism, which held that choice of candidates by conventions was undemocratic. A presidential primary, however, is a strange sort of election. Its results cannot be binding on the delegates in the maneuvering at the national convention. The choice given the voters who take part in the primaries—usually a small part of the electorate—sometimes does not include all the most important candidates. At best a presidential primary is a rough test of the popularity of certain candidates; and this function might be served more accurately by scientific sampling of voter opinion.

The primaries nevertheless are useful: they dramatize the choices that must be made. They serve at least part of the function intended for them by allowing candidates not favored by party leaders to prove themselves if they can. Estes Kefauver became known in the primaries and thus a formidable contender even though the party leadership did not support him. The primaries, moreover, are an opportunity to assess the importance of certain issues. Thus, John Kennedy demonstrated in the 1960 primaries, particularly West Virginia, that being Catholic was not a practical disqualification of his candidacy. Without this evidence behind him, he might well have failed in the national convention. The primaries do have some merits, then, despite their partial nature, their costliness, and their indecisiveness. Ultimately they winnow the serious and the promising candidates from the frivolous and the hopeless.

In other states delegates to the national conventions are chosen in state convention, a process involving primarily the professional politician. Personal connections between aspiring candidates and local leaders are at a premium. Though there is something discriminatory it should not be exaggerated; it is part of the political profession to be in touch with leaders in different localities, and a competent candidate will send emissaries to those states where he is not already known. The state conventions' incentive to select a winner minimizes the bias that may arise from purely personal friendship or antagonism. There is probably less emotionalism and more coldly rational assessment of candidates in the state conventions than in the primaries. Because the rational test applied is whether a candidate is likely to win, the ends of democracy are probably as well, if not better, served by the conventions. The general effect of using two modes of selecting delegates to the national conventions is to benefit from some of the advantages of each. On the whole the voice of the professional politicians comes out stronger.

All this is preliminary to the big show, the national conventions, which are perhaps the strangest working political bodies of the western world. Nowhere else has the art of organizing spontaneity been more highly developed, and yet somehow spontaneity in fact survives. Rational thinking is the last virtue to be expected from the mob scenes these conventions present; yet some clear thinking goes on. The noise is deafening yet men manage to be heard. Speeches are innumerable, endless, and banal, but some are terse and good. Little that occurs on the floor is to be taken at face value, but little is utterly without point either. A national convention at moments has the air of a nineteenth-century revivalist meeting, at times it is like a great sporting event, and sometimes a street riot.

To an observer it is a marvel that any sensible achievement emerges from the events, much less that any rationality operates. Yet there is a kind of rationality and invariably the results provide candidates acknowledged as those between whom the nation must choose at a general election. Usually, though not always, there results also a rough framing of a symbolic compromise among the many factions of the American people. Since these things do occur, it is tempting to assume that the real work of the convention goes on behind the scenes and the visible show is itself meaningless or the product of manipulation by backstage wire-pullers. In part this picture is true. There are innumerable hotel-room meetings, countless telephone calls, and covert, prearranged signaling. Many of these communications, however, are less hidden than the participants seem to believe and not infrequently the secrets are shared with millions who sit in fascination before their television sets. Some of the "secrets" are deliberately planted in order so to be revealed, but to a very considerable degree the supposedly devious maneuverings are open to public scrutiny. Intensive television coverage has made secrecy extremely difficult to maintain; indeed, it sometimes seems that the nationwide audience must be better informed as to what is occurring than many of the delegates at the conventions. For the rest, some of the crucial events appear on the floor in full session, beyond any hope of concealment. In the conventions at which an incumbent President is a candidate for re-election there is of course only the problem of simulating drama.

Some candidates arrive at a contested convention without elaborate organization and have little more of a plan than to be available in case of stalemate among the front-runners. Their chances are poor—no dark horse has been successful in recent times—but given the magnificence of the prize, hope springs eternal. The most serious candidates come well equipped. Probably none in history have been as meticulously prepared as John Kennedy in 1960 and Barry Goldwater in 1964. The Kennedy organization used strategically placed telephones on the floor, runners to bring messages where only footwork would serve, and even walkie-talkies. The planning for both of these men was minute and effective, foreseeing contingencies and with elaborate precautions even for unforeseen developments. How much these skills of modern organization accounted for is difficult to say, since each of these men was obviously in front before the conventions met.

The excitement of a convention often begins over the seating of challenged delegates. These contests may relate to purely internal state quarrels; they may also reflect fundamental issues that could split the party and endanger its hopes of success. The Democratic conventions have had more than their share of such contests in recent years, most connected with civil rights. While the Republicans have on the whole been spared this ordeal they may not be better off for having escaped it. As in many other spheres of American life, contest and even conflict sometimes confer benefits. The opening struggles give signs as to the way the winds are blowing in the party. The signs become clearer when the permanent chairman is chosen. The chairman's is not just a post of honor, for he can influence the outcome of events by his choice among the competing voices clamoring for recognition at critical moments.

With the convention organized, the nominating speeches begin. Some are fairly perfunctory, if anything about a convention can ever be perfunctory:—for favorite sons who have no hope but are deemed worthy of honor or serve merely to hold their delegation for bargaining purposes or some more devious plan. As the real candidates are put forward, an extraordinary ritual of nineteenth-century oratory rings forth. "The man who . . ." becomes an incantation repeated again and again as the description of the as yet unnamed Paladin mounts with rolling intensity and fervor, until the suspense can be carried no longer. Then with a great shout the orator gives the name of the hero he is nominating. With a great roar, the convention explodes as with surprise and delight, a wild parade erupts onto the aisles, and while the band plays and delegates cheer and noisemakers resound, the proceedings are brought to a halt. The process is repeated for each of the principal candidates, and gradually it begins to lose some of its synthetic drama. For connoisseurs, however, there are subtle differences in the length and apparent ardor of the various demonstrations. But these *cognoscenti* are few and nearly everyone simply enjoys the spectacle and showmanship of it all.

With the balloting things become serious. There are certain standard gambits but to a large extent they are attempts to build a bandwagon movement, or better yet a steamroller. The latter would be preferable: to get it over in the first balloting would obviously be more pleasant and more impressive. This, however, is not always a possibility. Then the art of holding back certain blocs to cast into the cauldron at a psychological moment and spread dismay into hostile ranks comes into its own. This specialized skill, like other esoteric arts, probably is less important than its practitioners would admit. Ultimately if indeed not early, the bandwagon appears and nothing can stop it. The laggard recognizes its approach, then makes a headlong scramble not to be left behind, and suddenly the convention is declaring its unanimity for the party's candidate.

What remains is anticlimax, although it is important. The vice presidency is by general accord now recognized as a matter of choice for the presidential nominee. Nevertheless, the choice is severely limited. If the struggle for the presidential nomination has been lively and touched with bitterness, there is a very strong reason to heal the wounds to party unity by choosing one of the defeated aspirants. The aspirant chosen, however, must represent a different core of strength than the successful nominee. Moreover, thought must be given to the presidential qualifications of the man chosen. All these considerations force the test of personal compatibility between the two nominees into a secondary position. Certainly John Nance Garner was less than soulmate for Franklin D. Roosevelt, and Lyndon B. Johnson was not an intimate to the Kennedy organization inner councils. Both of these combinations symbolized a bridge across the deepest geographical split in the nation. In all the madness of a convention then, there is rationality. It is the rationality shared by nearly all who take part, the logic of winning the coming election. This is selfish without question; it does, nonetheless, serve the important public function of formulating a broad compromise for the voting public to accept or reject.

Campaigning

The campaign begins on Labor Day. From then until the election the candidates drive themselves, and are driven by their commitments and their managers—which, if nothing else, tests their capacities for physical survival. This period is longer than electoral campaigns in Europe and critics regularly call for shorter campaigns. The voters, they claim, are bored; the costs are excessive and the whole affair is a pointless distraction from the serious matters of life. Perhaps the development of television campaigning and extensive press reporting have now permitted voters to form earlier impressions of the choices before them. Often, it is suggested, they have made up their minds long before election day. Yet this is not always true, for close elections would not necessarily yield the same results were they held a month or more earlier. Moreover, there is a partly justified general suspicion that the television medium is susceptible to its own kind of theatrical deception in that it carries favors for television performers who film well but who may not necessarily be the candidates who would succeed best in office. Moreover, the analogy with most European elections is poor. The American President represents the entire nation—directly. He is more than a party leader, and elected he becomes chief executive in his own right. Moreover, the magnitude of the United States at least creates a presumption that a campaign here is a greater undertaking.

The really important ground for hesitating to accept the reform of

a shorter campaign, however, is that the campaign experience is important background for a prospective President to have. The office has no
training ground as such and it is difficult to conceive that any curricu-
lum preparing for the presidency could ever be developed. In campaigning a candidate is not only making (or failing to make) an impact
on the voters, he is also exposing himself to all the diversity of the
nation, its concerns and moods. Travel about the land and contact with
great numbers of Americans insures some exposure to these concerns
and moods. The campaign is not ideal, but an adequate substitute
would be difficult to devise. Even where the candidate is an incumbent
President, it is highly useful that he renew his contact with those he
must lead and meet attacks of even the most interested and captious
sort.

If this service of the election campaign is commonly ignored or
undervalued, the other criticisms are on the whole misplaced. The
charge that campaigns are too expensive is usually without reference
point; the implication is that *all* money spent in campaigns is wasted.
This view is really part of the attitude that holds the work of politics
unimportant and lacking in seriousness. This attitude, of course, is seldom explicit and is irrationally combined with charges that the works
of politicians are dangerously mistaken. Those works are often of the
greatest importance, involving as they do the prospect of prosperity or
depression and peace or war. And if this is true, it is certainly wrong to
suggest that only small amounts should be spent on selecting a national
leader and in calling upon Americans to reflect upon their common
affairs; it is even more wrong to dismiss politics as pure waste of time.

Presidential campaigns differ from one another as circumstances
vary. A few persistent conditions nevertheless produce recurrent responses. First, where an incumbent President is running for re-election,
as on the whole he must if he is eligible, the campaign tends to revolve
about his record and his program. The incumbent has great advantages: he is inevitably better known; he is able to blur the distinction
between his role as chief executive of the nation and his role as party
nominee. His opponent is somehow guilty of bad taste, if not worse, in
some eyes for criticizing a national symbol. The incumbent President
need do and say nothing to reap this advantage; it is sufficient that he
quietly stress the importance of his tasks as national leader. This is
highly frustrating to his opponent but must be accepted. The incumbent President can refuse, quite rightly, to participate in television de-

bates and so avoid casting reflected fame upon his rival. Whether for these reasons or sheer tradition, incumbent Presidents can usually look forward to re-election.

Where neither candidate is an incumbent President, the advantages are less consistently on one side. The candidate whose party has held the presidency at the time of election may be able to cite the virtues of experience and intimacy with the problems of state, as Nixon did in 1960. This approach is available if the candidate has been a conspicuous member of the outgoing administration, but it is not a strong advantage. The candidate of the opposing party, on the other hand, can appeal to the accumulated hostilities generated by the party in power. As the American system has worked in the past, there is apparently a limit on the time one party may control the presidency without making too many enemies. This limit undoubtedly was reached in 1952, for example.

In our two parties are conditions peculiar to each. The most obvious is the long-term hold of the Democrats on "the solid South." Observers are now looking for the final dissolution of this historic accident. It may be said that the election of 1964 provided the break; yet the accompanying increase of Negro voting and the continuing hold of the Democratic party on Negro loyalty cast doubt on its ultimate significance. There are other areas where traditional loyalties go strongly to one party or the other: Vermont, for example, is a proverbially Republican state. These loyalties are very stubborn indeed; the political systems that develop in such states tend to perpetuate them. Nevertheless, it would be rash to say that they are beyond possible challenge.

Since the New Deal there has been something of a class difference in the core groups to which the major parties have strongest appeal. On the whole the Republicans retain the loyalties of business and the wealthier parts of the electorate, while the Democrats have the advantage with lower income groups and labor. It is easy to exaggerate this difference, which is not a polar factor, although it is real. To say that the Republicans have the money while the Democrats have the voters is a gross overstatement. The Democrats collect money, and the Republicans win elections. There are genuine differences between the two parties—matters of policy for example—but they are generally never diametric.

The really important fact is that, for whatever reasons, the Democrats have in recent times enjoyed a three to two lead over the Republicans in voter identification. Party identification is the significant factor in choosing a President, perhaps more so than the appeals of personality or issues. By this logic the Democrats ought to win consistently; they do not, of course, always win. People with large incomes and more education are more likely to vote than those with lower incomes and less education. Thus one apparent disadvantage of the Republicans is to some degree counterbalanced.

The basic difference in voter identification does bear on the strategies that underlie the campaigns of the two parties. The Democrats have all to gain normally by appealing to party loyalty. It can be combined with appeals to party principles, but the emphasis is that the candidate is a *Democratic* candidate. Thus the task of the Democrats is to get out the vote. If they succeed in marking their candidate as the party candidate and insure a large voter turnout they can reasonably expect to win. In contrast, the Republicans gain more by insisting that the campaign is between candidates and that the voters ought to choose the best man without regard to party. Their problem is to detach a substantial number of Democrats from the Democratic nominee while holding on to their own party identifiers; the former is more difficult. When a national hero like General Eisenhower is available, the Republican problem is most easily solved.

The matter of principles and policy is difficult for both parties. Each must, after all, look to a formulation of a majority of those who actually come to the polls. Clear statements on policy sometimes lose more votes than they gain. The Republican experience in 1964, when Senator Goldwater was especially forceful on a number of issues and when disaster struck at the polls, is unlikely to tempt either party to sharpen issues.

When, at long last, the election actually occurs, what is settled is very simply which man is going to be President and which party is going to have general influence over (*control of* is too strong) the executive branch of the government. The concurrent congressional and other elections are also influenced by the presidential election. But for the rest, what has been settled? In one sense very little and in another a great deal. The specific pledges made during the campaign that must be redeemed are usually few, and generally not vastly important. General Eisenhower's promise during his campaign to go to the Far East is as good an example of a specific pledge as can be found. It was, however, but a gesture—a token of intent to end the Korean War. In everyone's eyes the general intent was what counted, and it depended on more than a President's trip. Sometimes a claim is made that a winning candidate by virtue of his success has a "mandate" for a specific action. It can never be said that the voters intend some specific act. Yet there is a mandate to the President to carry the leadership of the nation. He has the authority of his constitutional powers as President, and to claim a mandate in any other sense is irrelevant and often a confession of weakness.

The Achievement

The most important question to be asked about the process is how well it actually serves its major ends. There have been moments in American history when the electoral system and its attendant parties seriously failed. The goal of maintaining a fundamental unity of the nation was not met in the campaign and election that gave Abraham Lincoln the presidency. The issues then before the nation could not be resolved by any process of compromise and accommodation; indeed, perhaps they were such that compromise and accommodation should not occur. In the election of 1892 the established party system failed markedly to encompass the demands of a large and seriously aggrieved segment of the population, the farmers. A new party, the Populists, appeared and demonstrated the strength and intensity of the farmer grievances so that in the following campaign account was taken of them. It is at least arguable that the system was deaf to the grievances of workingmen during the first part of this century. It is impossible to say how close the country came to domestic upheaval in the depths of the Great Depression. But certainly it was a time of danger, which registered in 1932, and the political process has never been blind in this way since.

Failures such as those in 1860, 1892 and the twentieth century are more important than the deficiencies of style that our electoral campaigns regularly exhibit. The process of picking a President is noisy, undignified, and often absurd. Purists may well wish for more graceful campaigning, more incisive and more intellectually elevated debates. Quite possibly, however, achieving these desirable conditions might rob the process of much of its vitality and leave the ultimate winner with no accurate sense of the temper of the American people. A presidential election is, above all, an articulation of the mood of the electorate. It is by no means an ideal device, but it would be difficult to contrive a more accurate and more meaningful one.

A presidential election and all the process of which it is the quadrennial culmination is a vital part, probably the most vital part, of the life of American democracy. Its essential quality is compromise, compromise among the myriad elements that make up a nation of continental expanse. This accommodation is a continuing matter, but the existing balance is brought under thoroughgoing review every four years, and the differences reduced to a choice between two candidates for the presidency. The ultimate test is that the outcome be accepted as valid by the American people. With one exception, this validation has been given. The President, his opponent, and their supporting parties are the essential means for posing this regular test and precipitating the review by which it is passed.

Chapter III

PRESIDENT

AND CONGRESS

Much that is crucial to American political life revolves about the relationship between the President and the Congress. When the framers of the Constitution established them as coordinate branches of the new government, they undoubtedly considered that they were merely giving explicit recognition to a fundamental principle of government: that these two branches reflected two inherently different functions. The intricately contrived system of checks and balances they added set the stage for a recurrent drama in American history, the contest between the two departments.

Separation of powers, especially the legislative and the executive, is often cited as a basic principle of American government. Whatever the vision of the founders, in actuality this principle has proved secondary to federalism, which the founders themselves hammered out with great originality. The President and the Congress both represent the nation; together they provide the authentication of policy and the consent without which popular government, perhaps government itself, could not exist in the United States. They work, however, in utterly different ways. Partly they differ in their activities of legislation and administration; but more important they represent the nation in different ways.

The President represents the nation as a whole, while the Congress represents it as a collection of states and congressional districts. The separation of the powers of the executive and the legislative is the embodiment of federalism. Inevitably, because of the different constituencies of the President and of the various senators and congressmen, a President is often sharply at odds with the views and purposes of many of the men of Capitol Hill. It would be comforting to assume that the many different positions that congressmen and senators take add up together to a position as national and as public-spirited as the President's, yet often the two branches arrive at quite different positions. Which then is correct? Which more surely represents the people of the United States? It is difficult to predict which will prove *wiser*. As to which is more public-spirited, the answer is also ambiguous. Insofar as both President and Congress respond to the wishes of the public (which both do more than they are given credit for), it is hard to show one branch is better than the other.

In the degree to which they prefer *national* interests, however, there is a significant distinction. The men of the Hill represent different publics, different from each other's and from the President's. Their constituencies are vastly different, some consisting largely of farmers, some of large cities, some of working-class districts, some of states where mining is overwhelmingly important, and so on; but the President's constituency consists of all of the people. Because the smaller constituencies emphasize particular interests, the aggregate representation offered by Congress does not equal that of the presidency. The consequence is that there is consistently some difference between the policy positions of Congress and the President. On the whole, the President tends to emphasize national considerations and the interests of a great diversity of people more often than Congress. This is not to say that his position will necessarily always be "better"; not only can he make errors, but national interests, the interests that are most widely shared, should not always be utterly preferred to particular interests.

It is firmly in the American tradition to protect minorities. Nevertheless, it is true that very large differences of outlook are built into the government.

A Shifting Relationship

Although the tension between President and Congress is a persistent characteristic of the American government system, the locus of power has oscillated significantly between the two. Perhaps the most striking shift came with the death of Lincoln. During the Civil War he acted independently of Congress with near contempt. Congress struck back during the war, but was not really effective until after he was gone from the scene. In a very short period, the leaders of Congress virtually seized power and subjected Lincoln's successor to the worst humiliation any President has ever had to endure, impeachment proceedings. Congressional power was so firmly established that several decades later it was entirely appropriate for a young scholar, Woodrow Wilson, to characterize the American pattern in the title of his first book as "congressional government," government, that is, by the standing committees of the House of Representatives. Wilson later had to revise his estimate.

These changes were neither the first nor the last of the oscillations. Indeed, the first came with the adoption of the Constitution itself. The very creation of the presidency marked a recession from the mistrust of the executive that had been passed on from the hatred of the English king. In view of the subsequent development of relations between President and Congress, it is curious that much of the dislike of legislatures stemmed from a sense that they were too popular, too democratic an element in the pattern. Just as Jefferson had begun to make the presidency into something of a popular organ, however, Congress reasserted itself and until Jackson's presidency there was, as one writer has put it, a period of "congressional sovereignty." Jackson broke this condition by his sheer force of personality and his exercise of party leadership. The presidency thus definitely assumed the role of popular advocate it has largely held since.

Before Lincoln assumed his nearly dictatorial powers there was another strong renewal of congressional power vis-à-vis the presidency. Buchanan may have been weak in his personal qualifications, but certainly the congressional opposition he met would have frustrated a more able and determined President. This record undoubtedly reinforced Lincoln's disinclination to go to Congress for authority before acting.

On the whole, national crises have been the times of greatest growth in presidential as against congressional power. This growth has been most apparent in time of war, but it was also true during the Great Depression of the thirties. The executive has greater capacity for action and bears a continuing responsibility, and so it is not mere coincidence. Nevertheless, in the oscillation of the preponderance of power several other factors are important. First, a period of congressional dominance creates problems that in time must be solved and on which popular demands insist action be taken. Such problems and such demands were building up throughout the latter part of the nineteenth-century period of "congressional government." Thus, for example, the widespread distress on the farms got but little effective attention from government in this time. Thus also the attack upon monopoly was half-hearted and ineffectual. Such problems helped produce the actionist mood of Theodore Roosevelt and provided the basis for the program of Woodrow Wilson.

There is also the striking fact that, as Wilfred Binkley has observed, there has been a consistent difference between the sorts of Presidents the two major parties have produced. To a remarkable degree, the Democratic Presidents have been strong while the Republican Presidents on the whole have been weak. In part the difference is the work of chance, that Democratic Presidents have come to office in times of crisis more often than have Republicans. In greater part, however, the difference lies in a greater preference of the Democratic Party for strong Presidents. However fashionable it may be to emphasize the similarities between the two parties, here is a major point of difference between them.

It is difficult to establish just what the systems of belief underlying the difference in preference are. It is possible to point to the beliefs of particular Presidents, however. Thus Woodrow Wilson had a vision of an American system of government similar to the British; and Britain, of course, has no separation of powers. Certainly Wilson did not hesitate to press Congress for measures he felt desirable. It is accordingly ironic that the ultimate failure of his career, the rejection of the League of Nations, was a failure of his relations with the legislative branch.

Other modern Democratic Presidents have shown great willingness to extract from Congress every last measure they could. The opening period of Franklin D. Roosevelt's New Deal is the classic example. During the "hundred days," he sent measure after measure to Congress, which dutifully enacted them, sometimes even before printed copies of the bills were available for consideration. Yet like Wilson, Roosevelt ultimately misjudged the limits of what as President he could accomplish with Congress. He attempted far too much with his scheme for changing the composition of the Supreme Court and came out severely bloodied and with an impaired reputation. When he sought to intervene in congressional elections to remove his congressional opponents (the "purge" of 1938), the results were so meager as to be a failure.

More recent Democratic Presidents may have learned from their predecessors' experiences, but the lessons have in no way diminished their desire to play highly active roles in the legislative process. Harry Truman was obviously in a weaker position than FDR; the war was over, the country's mood was more conservative, the Congress was Republican, and he himself lacked the Roosevelt voice and manner. Yet he made strenuous efforts to get the congressional action he wanted, and when he failed he ran his campaign for re-election not against the Republican nominee for President but against the record of the Eightieth Congress, which had obstructed him. It was a successful tactic.

John F. Kennedy was perhaps the most cautious of the Democratic Presidents. His short time in office probably exaggerates the impression of caution he left and his slender margin of electoral victory undoubtedly checked his impulse to action. Yet he was at every point acutely aware of the difficulties he faced at the opposite end of Pennsylvania Avenue, so aware that he pressed for his program with less vigor than a more insensitive President might have used. Despite these limitations of situation and temperament, however, he had a vision of legislative responsibilities very like his predecessors'. In fact, his contribution was probably felt in the successful outcome of Lyndon Johnson's extreme activism with Congress, a forcefulness that may prove to have few matches in presidential history.

The recent Republican Presidents present a marked contrast. Herbert Hoover had the worst luck of any President since Andrew Jackson. Much of his meager record must be set down to the brutal fact of the Great Depression's arrival and his defeat for re-election. Nevertheless, both by temperament and belief he was ill disposed to place much pressure on Congress. In personality, he had little of the superficial grace and appeal that help disarm opposition. In belief, he was committed to avoiding public action wherever possible; he had a strong distaste for laws and anything that smacked of compulsion. Dwight Eisenhower held an even more rigid view of his place as President. At times he seemed to envisage an almost absolute separation between the executive and the legislative functions; the former were his but they should in no way intrude upon the functions of Congress. He was, of course, not consistent in this apparent view—no President possibly could be—but it is certain that he had a very exalted view of the prerogatives of Congress. He endured attacks from Senator McCarthy upon his department with a silent patience that astonished his contemporaries. Ultimately his behavior is traceable only to a belief that a President should not mix in legislative affairs.

The Intricacies of Government's Concerns

If there are considerable differences in the conceptions of the President's proper role in legislation as held by the major parties and by different Presidents, these differences are of degree relating only to the question of how active should the President be in the legislative process? Even President Eisenhower, who took as nearly extreme a position of presidential passivity vis-à-vis Congress as any modern President, was often a genuine activist in practice. The time is now past when a President could leave law-making to the legislators. The President today and henceforth is, whether he likes it or not, the chief law-maker. One fundamental reason is, as Edward S. Corwin observed, "the revival of legislation of national scope"—and the imperative need for it. Behind this need lies the steadily intensifying integration of the nation. In the past Congress could pass measures designed purely to assist particular regions, states, or localities confident that the effects would reach only the particular areas. Accordingly, the bulk of legislation could be left to the bargaining and logrolling of the representatives from the affected areas; thus questions of reclamation or arid lands could reasonably be left to the senators and congressmen from the western states, cotton matters could be placed in the hands of legislators from the cotton states, and so on. A strong tradition still prevails that most legislative problems should be handled in this manner. It was probably never true that even cotton and reclamation were of such exclusively regional concern as their handling in Congress suggested, but today these and most problems plainly have important national implications. The nation is more closely knit each year; communications steadily improve, and both economically and socially the nation becomes more nearly one. The President, with his unique constituency of that nation, is forced to regard most legislation as national legislation—and to take an active part in its formulation and passage.

The increasing intricacy of national organization of all kinds is paralleled by a similar integration internationally. Accordingly, some of the most important foreign problems requiring legislation have a character that inescapably places them on the President's desk. Foreign affairs have always been of this nature. Today, however, they have an almost bewildering complexity and few congressmen or senators can safely devote themselves to acquiring expertise here. Even for those few who can, the nature of the problems and the information needed make this area the peculiar province of the executive branch.

Another such area is monetary policy. This abstruse field is too technical for more than a few of the legislative representatives, but all of them have a keen sense of its deep importance to the health of the general economy. Congress has attempted to place a major part of this policy area in the hands of an independent body, the Federal Reserve Board, where it presumably is invulnerable to presidential or partisan whims. Despite occasional minor collisions of executive and Board policies, however, general monetary policy on the whole is managed beyond the effective reach of Congress but not beyond the President's. Closely related to monetary policy in general significance is fiscal (tax) policy. Here by contrast Congress has always felt itself both competent and constrained to take an active part. Yet, increasingly as Keynesian economics have gained the day, executive influence has been prominent, and is likely to grow. Much the same is true in areas such as military and scientific policy. Congress may react in dismay from time to time, but it is inevitably in an inferior position compared with the executive. And the President is the Chief Executive.

Presidential Legislation

Important as is the change resulting from the increasing complexities of modern life, even more is the deep and subtle change that has come over the government itself. It is a form of technological change. To understand it, it is necessary to look back a number of decades. Up until the end of World War I there was nothing whatever that could be taken as a general plan of government programs and operations. Congress, jealously guarding its duties and prerogatives on taxing and spending, passed bills and appropriations separately, without regard to the relationship of each piece of legislation to the other. This practice would in a business firm or a household soon bring disaster. Although it did not bring disaster to the nation, it was costly and wasteful. In 1921 a fundamental reform of American government was passed, the Budget and Accounting Act. While the major impetus was the drive to bring expenditures and income into some sensible relationship to each other, the Act's long-term importance was more far-reaching. It called upon the President to prepare an annual budget to present to Congress. While Congress undertook neither to accept the budget nor to refrain from tampering with it (and in practice has proved ready to make large-scale changes), passage of the Act was a profound admission that Congress was incapable of serving this fundamental function of government; the job went where it had to rest, to the executive branch.

The effective reform, however, was years in the making. The Bureau of the Budget was only gradually able to do more than collect and add up the various separate demands for money and to tabulate the various sources of income. Moreover, until 1939 the Budget Bureau was located in the Treasury, when it went to the Executive Office of the President. The new location and the growing competence and prestige of the Bureau not only enhanced its power, they markedly increased the President's capability. This increased capability extended to most parts of government in one degree or another—and gave the President a great advantage over Congress. He now had a basic tool for making the executive branch his own (as indeed the Constitution indicated it should be, but as previous practice had never allowed). Congress could still change particular features of his plan and enforce its own authority over particular agencies, but the Budget, increasingly the President's plan, was the starting point.

Over the years it has become apparent that the creation of the Bureau of the Budget was no mere administrative reform directed to housekeeping tidiness; it was a governmental change of constitutional importance. A fundamental device for coordinating policy, it placed both power and responsibility for policy on the President. The change effected was not apparent during World War II, a period in which executive leadership in legislation was to be expected anyhow, or even immediately afterward. In 1946, for example, one complaint was that there was no legislative program coming from the President: presidential reports and recommendations, yes, but no presidential legislative program as such. Later, under President Truman, however, just such a program took form, and under President Eisenhower, who often seemed to defer to Congress in his general statements, the formulation of a President's program became both routinized and accepted.

With the new Republican administration firmly established after some inevitable initial groping, the Bureau of the Budget, acting in the President's name, sent instructions in mid-1954 to all the federal agencies calling for them to submit legislative plans according to a standard form. Out of the intense scrutiny of the resulting mass of agency proposals by the topmost leadership of the new Republican administration the President's legislative program emerged. As Richard Neustadt observed, the development of this program was less an innovation by President Eisenhower than the product of bureaucratic momentum, which carried on a beginning made during the previous administration. It was also the natural evolution of the change that started in 1921.

Although this change is of vast importance to the character of the American government system, it should not be regarded as a total transformation. As we have seen, it has been in progress for more than four decades and has involved both Republican and Democratic administrations. And although the trend is quite clear retrospectively, the President and the executive branch under him have not reduced Congress to a rubber stamp. When a great majority in Congress is of the same party as the President, as emerged from the election of 1964, the President may briefly have his way to a striking degree. This situation is inevitably short-lived, however; party discipline is weak and the highly touted persuasive powers of even a Lyndon Johnson cannot maintain the harmony (or subservience, according to some) of Congress with the President's desires. Moreover, a shrewd President will inevitably tailor his program to what he conceives is possible; he may desire much more far-reaching legislation than he sends to Congress, but he will certainly have no desire to incur a series of defeats that may damage his prestige.

Despite this ground for presidential caution, however, the fact remains that an important change has occurred. There has been a gradual but widespread acceptance of the concept of a presidential program of legislation. While it is understood, as it has been for a long time, that the formulation of measures must take place in the individual agencies of the executive branch, it is now also accepted that the important measures of the President's program be drafted in the Bureau of the Budget, which has particularly competent facilities for this function. This is far from saying that Congress will accept the measures, or even accord them a high degree of respect. At the same time, Congress has become reluctant to pass measures that touch on subjects of interest to the President but do not have executive support. Such bills are not likely to receive favored treatment at all the checkpoints along the road to passage by Congress. Leading senators will even on occasion refer proposed measures to the executive branch for initial decision and possible bill drafting by the Bureau of the Budget. This is very different from the operation of the separation of powers as it has traditionally been pictured.

Although there is no single formal presentation of the President's legislative program to Congress, each year three highly important general messages go from the President to Congress. The first is the State of the Union Message, the only regular message called for by the Constitution. It provides the President with an opportunity to discuss general matters and outline his program, and to dramatize it, if he desires, by his personal appearance before the two Houses. It is not the proper vehicle for laying bare all the measures and details which he will later send to Congress. The second is the Budget Message, which is accompanied by the massive volume containing the Budget itself. The third is the Economic Report. This, the newest, dates from passage of the Employment Act of 1946, a measure whose full importance is just now becoming apparent. The Act, which was based on the deep change in economic thinking associated with the name of John Maynard Keynes, made it a matter of national policy to maintain the national economic health as measured by employment. It is accompanied by the Report of the Economic Advisors, and states the major economic problems facing the nation and indicates the thinking underlying the administration's general economic policy. For the rest, there are now other messages, special in the sense of covering particular topics such as conservation or housing, but general in that they do not detail the various measures which will follow. During the first few months of the new session, Congress may well feel that it is being loaded with an overwhelming agenda by the President.

Legislative Party Organization

If the President sets much of the agenda of Congress, what follows is very much in the hands of Congress. Each senator and each congressman is a power in his own right; he has been elected by his constituents and is responsible directly to them. He is not an appointee of the President and cannot be removed by the President. However much he may admire the President and believe in his program, each senator and representative feels a more or less strong compulsion to assert his independence and autonomy against the White House. At times he may appear arrogant or downright cussed, but this is the direct reflection of his election by a distinct constituency; refusal to assert independence could well be taken as subservience and misrepresentation of the folks back home. This factor occasionally produces ludicrous results, as when senators address each other as though each were the high plenipotentiary of a proud and haughty nation. Once in a while this spirit of independence takes exaggerated form so that an individual senator becomes a veritable wild cell, with disastrous consequences to both government and nation. Fortunately, however, the Huey Longs and the Joseph McCarthys are rare.

Partly because of the autonomy inherent in the position of senator or congressman, many checks have developed to prevent Congress from flying off into bits. Perhaps the most important of these checks is the most general and diffuse—what may be termed the corporate spirit of each house. It is very marked in the Senate, which has often been described as a club. A large number of customs and rules, both formal and informal, circumscribe the behavior of the members. Thus, for example, a new member is expected to remain quiet and inconspicuous until after sufficient time has elapsed for him to know all the niceties. Similarly, no member is allowed to impugn the motives of others. There are many such rules and almost all of them are grounded in the common awareness of the possibility of disastrous results to all if the members exercise their independence to the full. There is a further clear understanding that if any member is to achieve results for his own constituency, he has to gain the support of other members of his house. He cannot afford their hostility and has everything to gain by earning the gratitude of others. Nor would it be realistic to assume that senators and congressmen lack concern for the national interest.

The other large restraint upon independence is the party system. Sometimes, when a popular President elected by a large majority has brought into Congress a substantial number of his own party on his coattails, the winning party may seem irresistible, and sweep all before it in Congress. Apprehensive voices assert that the American system of government has been destroyed and that inevitably the President as leader of his party will enforce strict discipline in Congress and thereby wipe out the separation between the executive and legislative branches. For a time the results may seem to bear out the alarmist cries: this is the way things seemed to Republican critics in the early days of the New Deal and many have seen it in the years immediately following Johnson's huge victory over Goldwater. At such moments, the American pattern resembles the British, with party discipline placing government power, both executive and legislative, in the hands of the national leader.

Such a picture, however, is seriously overdrawn. The periods during which this situation has prevailed have been few indeed. In 1934 Franklin Roosevelt was able to have his way with Congress not merely because he had so many fellow Democrats in Congress, but because the country was in a state of crisis. In any clear and obvious crisis, partisans of both labels rally behind the President as the national leader. When the astonishing growth of the Democratic majority occurred in the election of 1936, a growth directly attributable to the popularity of the President, relations between President and Congress nevertheless became decidedly sticky. There followed the 1938 "purge" attempt, a venture from whose effects cooperative relations between the two branches were restored only by the new crisis of World War II. As for the fears of presidential domination supposedly inherent in the "consensus" proclaimed by President Johnson and apparently authenticated by Congress after his victorious sweep in the election of 1964, their substance related mainly to another war; legislative subservience otherwise began to erode.

Party discipline in the United States is a presidential weapon with only limited reliability. The times a President can appeal to his own party's congressional organization to gain passage of measures otherwise doomed are limited. As with almost any weapon a large part of the utility of discipline depends on its being used sparingly. This is a major consideration formulating that peculiar category of presidentially supported measures, the "must" bills. In the two houses of Congress, party discipline is really quite weak, sometimes nonexistent. Moreover, the party organization in Congress, although it carries the name of the President's party, of which he is the official leader, is not the President's own organization. It is quite capable of dragging its feet and the President must frequently cajole or even threaten it; the threats are likely to be measures of desperation when used. One student, James M. Burns, has suggested that the congressional party organizations and the organizations headed by the President and his opposing party leader are so distinct that we have in effect a national politics of four rather than two parties, two of them presidential and two congressional. While a President cannot always rely on members of his own party for consistent support of his program in Congress, frequently members of the opposition do come to his support. President Eisenhower often benefited from the aid given by the Senate Democratic Leader Lyndon Johnson; Presidents Kennedy and Johnson similarly benefited from the help of Senate Republican Leader Everett M. Dirksen.

If such relationships are measured against a British model in which the government governs and the opposition opposes, we have chaos indeed. But the British model is not wholly relevant to American political reality. No American President expects to dominate Congress, nor does the machinery exist for him to do so; certainly party organization is very poorly adapted for such an attempt. A senator or congressman probably owes only a small debt to the President or the national party organization for his election. The party organization that participates in the election of a senator or a congressman (if, indeed, one exists) is a local or a state organization. Central party organizations may provide money for particular congressional candidates facing crisis, but for the most part resources must be found locally. On the whole these candidates have little reason for gratitude or dependence on national party organizations. And, man by man, they are unable to forget that each of their electorates is different from the next, most of all from that which chooses a President. After election, the candidates elected under the same party banner as the President may feel a share in the glory surrounding his name, but time quickly dulls the sense of obligation, and the competing obligation to the demands of the particular constituencies asserts itself. The initial cohesiveness of the winning party loosens, and the President finds that his party's congressional battalions are no longer his to command.

Special Interests and Groups

In dealing with Congress, indeed with virtually all of government, any President comes inevitably and repeatedly into collision with another feature of American political life. This is the very widespread existence of a multitude of organizations, some formal and some informal, each clustered about particular matters of policy or potential policy. It is the modern form of what James Madison termed the problem of "faction." The aspect of the problem that has received attention is lobbying; however, Presidents have always been vexed by the persistent and importuning influences of lobbyists seeking to gain their ends at the expense of presidential policy. In 1913 President Wilson, for example, felt called to issue a strong statement denouncing the horde of lobbyists who descend on Washington at the first whisper of new tariff legislation. Other Presidents have echoed him, and not just on tariff matters. While the activities of some lobbyists have on occasion assisted presidential programs and while a function of White House staff assistants is to act as lobbyists (or more politely, to serve as liaison with Congress), lobbyists have very generally helped to frustrate presidential ends.

Lobbying, however, is only one aspect of the problem, and certainly not the most important. Lobbying is in itself not wrong, nor, indeed, is there anything about it to which a President can properly take exception. The First Amendment to the Constitution guarantees the right to petition the government for a redress of grievances. Congress and the executive branch both would be severely handicapped if they could not draw on information and opinion from the citizenry. Moreover, the vision of Congressmen as passively responding to whatever pressures the lobbyists of "special interests" bring to bear is quite mistaken. While no Congressman would say that he ignores the statements of lobbyists, all Congressmen would indignantly reject any suggestion that they simply yield to pressure.

The real problem is quite different. Whether pressure is effective or not, it is usually unnecessary. Each congressman (and, to a lesser extent, each senator) is chosen by and represents a constituency that is smaller than the President's. Necessarily, the congressman's constituency has less diversity than the President's. Some indeed, include little more than a single preponderant economic interest, a particular farm commodity or a particular industry. In such a constituency or in one with few interests, there is little point in applying pressure on the elected representative; he will be keenly aware of the situation and may be relied upon to seek advice from the interest in question. Such a representative is not a lobbyist, but he usually does the work of the lobbyists much more effectively. As a consequence, the interests of such products as cotton, oil, apples, airplanes, and many others have especially good representation in Congress. In a national context, however, the voices of individual interests are much less resounding and often their echoes are drowned out in the competing clamor of the others.

Though there are hence great differences in the preoccupations of different congressmen and senators, to a large degree they do not conflict. Accordingly, the problem of the differences of concern can be easily solved by cooperative exchange of support for each others' projects—in short, by logrolling. The process is best typified by the Rivers and Harbors bills regularly passed by Congress. One congressman's concern may be limited to obtaining a levee for his district, while another may care only for a dam for *his* district, and so on. The general consequence, however, is likely to be a vast miscellany of projects unrelated to each other or, indeed, to the national interest. This process is repeated many times over in each legislative session; it produces peace among the most vociferous and powerful interests as well as among the legislators. It does not meet the needs for coherent plans of policy in public works, taxation, foreign affairs, or many other areas where the President is obliged by his mandate to have a large view.

To a substantial degree the organization within Congress is based upon the mutual accommodation of a variety of very separate interests. Such organization, though shifting with the needs and chances of alliance and support, is real and on the whole antagonistic to the very conception of a presidential program. It tends to elevate interests and values that are more solidly organized and more surely founded on the accidents of legislative district boundaries. This form of organization goes beyond the houses of Congress and includes particular agencies and bureaus of the executive branch as well as private organizations. Though often transitory, it can be durable and largely invulnerable to successful challenge. The committees of Congress, which so disturbed Woodrow Wilson when he was a student in the latter part of the nineteenth century, by their specialization and tendency to give inordinate power over certain fields of policy to congressmen from districts where those interests are especially strong, accentuate these systems of power. A President who proposes to challenge any of these systems must either be very strong or highly unwary.

Measures of Presidential Success

In face of this condition, the possibilities for presidential action involving Congress are severely limited. To measure presidential success by comparing the bills sponsored by one President that pass with those successfully sponsored by another may impart the kind of objectivity that comes with citing numbers. In a large sense, however, it is a false measure. Any politician acute enough to have risen to the presidency is keenly aware of the obstacles to his program in Congress. He will accordingly cut his program to the possibilities. While one President may, like Lyndon Johnson, have an unusual skill in persuasiveness and legislative generalship, his achievement will be only marginally enhanced by these attributes. Much, probably most, of what a President does not achieve with Congress consists of what he does not attempt. And for this there is no satisfactory measure.

Moreover, the achievement of a President in producing changes through legislative action is also understated by any tabulation of bills passed and failed in any one session. Although measures that require legislative sanction are usually important, they are not all equally important. And the major items of change never are accomplished in any single session of Congress. Although on a given date Congress may have taken final action on a particular measure, the day it passed was only the culmination of a process, invariably begun many years before and probably including defeats of earlier bills to the same end. Most of the really important legislation that has made history in recent years thus originated in earlier studies, education, and herculean effort—even decades before. The National Labor Relations Act, Social Security, Civil Rights, and Medicare are examples. A President who sponsors an important innovation but does not see it enacted in his own time may have made a greater contribution than the President under whose leadership it actually becomes law.

Although the fate of the President's legislative program is the most conspicuous index of the relations between President and Congress, other aspects are also important. One is the degree of cooperation or lack of it on foreign policy, an area by its nature peculiarly within the Presidential sphere. Congress, nevertheless, has a share in foreign policy. The most obvious part of this is the Senate's constitutional power to approve treaties. The Senate's rejection of American participation in the League of Nations will be vivid for years to come. Yet this memory exaggerates the probability that the Senate will again so repudiate a President. Partly because no President, recalling that event, would expose himself as Woodrow Wilson did, but partly also because the Senate is also unlikely to court the risks to the nation that comparable action in today's dangerous world might involve, the Senate probably has less power in foreign affairs than in the past. A prudent President, however, involves influential senators in the formulation—and sometimes the execution—of major steps in foreign affairs.

Similarly, Congress is capable of making life miserable for officials of the executive branch on whom the President may heavily depend. Congressional investigations have been seriously abused in the past for this purpose. A President may assert executive privilege in forbidding his appointees to testify before such investigations, but this defense may have only limited usefulness, as the story of Sherman Adams suggests. Adams, as President Eisenhower's chief assistant, aroused much hostility both by his manner and by his power. The President attempted to defend him against charges of using his office to gain favors for a friend, but eventually he had to permit his resignation to protect the reputation of the presidency. Eisenhower was thus compelled to choose between protecting a valuable assistant and maintaining his capacity to govern. Another device available to the Senate is refusal to approve a President's key appointment. It is an obviously hostile step that the Senate is genuinely reluctant to take. The threat to curtail appropriations for programs dear to a President's heart but run by men unpleasing to Congress is an almost constant problem for all Presidents.

Presidents, on the other hand, have weapons for any guerrilla war with Congress that may develop. They may veto bills displeasing to them. This power, which the framers of the Constitution stressed considerably, has been rarely used in recent years. If the bill vetoed carries provisions of serious matter to the constituents of leading senators or congressmen, it may cause genuine hostility. Although Franklin Roosevelt found the veto useful for imposing discipline, it is dangerous in lesser hands. Similarly, a President still controls some federal patronage. Usually "courtesy" demands that senators and congressmen be "consulted" (i.e., deferred to) in patronage appointments, but sometimes Presidents use appointments as weapons against maverick legislators. Much the same thing can be done with the location of defense plants and the placement of important contracts. A President may also make a stirring appeal over the head of Congress to the electorate by radio and television, a tactic which loses its effectiveness if used too often. All of these devices risk future retaliation and so can only be used with great restraint.

The relationship between President and Congress, then, is considerably different from that formally drawn in the great scheme of the Constitution. The separation of powers between these two branches has not indeed been removed; a vast gap separates the two. Nevertheless, the increasing complexities of modern political life have required an increasing role for the President, and the presidency has increasingly become institutionalized. Correlatively, the legislative branch has become less and less capable of mastering the daily flow of events of which policy is so largely composed; it is compelled to leave much to the executive branch. If present trends were to be projected into the future, we could envision a government system in which the President with the whole executive branch under his effective control governs, and Congress checks and criticizes. Already, this picture accords with what happens in some areas of policy, military and foreign affairs for example.

But this has not yet become a general pattern and it is far from clear that it ever will. Congress wields an enormous and active power. The manner of selecting its membership inevitably leads it into differences and occasionally collision with the presidency. Though Congress may be more and more handicapped by a growing gap of information and expertise in confrontations with the executive branch and find increasing difficulty in intelligently checking the actions of government, its capacity for checking and interfering does not seem likely to disappear. This prospect offers serious danger in the future, and can be mitigated only by restrained and responsible statesmanship on both sides.

The principal problem of the relationship between President and Congress continues to be what it has consistently been through most of American history; the difference between the constituent bases of the two. The one branch will persistently be drawn to look at the common needs of the nation as a whole, the other will as persistently be compelled to look to the particular wants of parts of the nation. The danger is not presidential domination of the legislative branch. Rather "it is because in their hours of timidity the Congress becomes subservient to the importunities of organized minorities that the President comes more and more to stand as the champion of the rights of the whole country." The author of this radical statement was that well-known presidential tyrant, Calvin Coolidge.

Chapter IV

PRESIDENT AND

EXECUTIVE

The President is the Chief Executive. This statement is founded on the clear and forthright first sentence of Article II of the Constitution: "The executive power shall be vested in a President of the United States of America." It also relates to the injunction that he shall take care that the laws be faithfully executed. These provisions, and a common and oversimplified view of the separation of powers, conjure up the vision of American government where Congress passes the laws and the President, commanding his subordinates, executes them. The vision is seriously mistaken as to what actually happens in the passage of laws, and it is equally inaccurate as to what happens in their execution. The reality, in fact, is so complex that it is now often difficult to speak meaningfully about "the executive branch." Not only does that branch, as we have seen, take significant leadership in legislation, but it is so divided, so fragmented, and its parts are often so autonomous that the President's power of command over them is often little more than a fiction. On the other hand, if checks upon presidential power are sought, they can be found as readily among these fragments as in Congress.

The powers of the President under the Constitution are great but at many points imprecisely defined. The courts have been reluctant to define his power more sharply; the courts, after all, are themselves the third of the great branches supposedly coordinate under the separation of powers. Nevertheless, they have given a handful of decisions that have placed some limitations on what Presidents may do. The most dramatic of these was the *Youngstown* decision of 1952; it compelled President Truman to undo his seizure of the steel mills in the face of a threatened strike by the steelworkers. Truman assumed he had power to do this under ambiguous legislation in combination with his general responsibilities as President. His position emphasized the great discretion inescapable in the presidency, and the Supreme Court felt obliged to strike down what seemed a dangerous claim. Even with this seemingly straightforward action, however, its meaning and future effect are still disputed. In a striking earlier case, *In re Neagle*, the existence of a fundamental power in the presidency to do what is necessary for the "execution" of the laws, here to injure the personal safety of judges, was affirmed but under such complicated circumstances and in such terms as to leave a deep uncertainty as to how far that power might reach.

The Executive Machinery

Probably the most important "executive" power of the President in our modern bureaucratized era is his power to direct the vast machinery of the executive branch. The courts have provided a few limitations, one of the more important relating to the President's power of removal of federal officials. This authority seems part of the power to command or direct and to flow from the vesting of the "executive power" in the President. It is clearly established, however, that the President may not easily remove a member of the important independent regulatory commissions. But the really big limitation comes from other sources. The most important is the great extension of the merit civil service. Federal employees under this system, the overwhelming majority of all public servants, can be removed only for narrowly prescribed offenses, and these do not include simple presidential displeasure. The threat of removal is largely meaningless anyhow, given the need for maintaining public services and the dependence of government on the expertise of officials.

There remains a very serious problem of maintaining responsibility of government in the executive branch. The President is the single elective official (except for the Vice President) in the executive branch and the essential medium of responsibility. Where law prescribes precisely what public servants must do, when there are standards of practice either of long standing or derived from scientific findings, the President is largely absolved from blame if the results prove unpopular. Yet many actions clearly rest on value decisions by administrators. These value decisions are choices—preferences—which have to stand as such. Who is to get the benefits and who the deprivations following from decisions? What kind of benefits are to be chosen, material or nonmaterial? Where such choices are mixed into the decisions of administration—and they are much more frequent than administrators usually care to admit—they must be justified somehow as reflecting the choices of the people themselves and not simply as those personally preferred by the officials. Since an appointive administrator has his only formal link with the people via his political superiors and finally the chief executive, the President is crucial in the formal scheme of responsible government, especially as the complexities of modern life require more of these decisions to be made by expert administrators.

In practice an administrator faced with an important decision that reflects a choice between values and between different interests will attempt to protect himself against the wrath of those who feel injured by his choices. He may disguise the existence of personal preference in his decision and insist that purely technical considerations prevailed; he may try to assess the sentiment of the people most obviously affected; certainly he will give thought to the relative strength of the various groups involved. In doing all this he may indeed establish some more or less formal means of consultation, an advisory committee, a conference, or other device. The result is hailed as the work of "democratic" administration, but the process's main end is to protect exposed administrators fearful of facing a legitimate charge of arbitrary behavior in exercising their own preferences. By mobilizing the support of those groups that benefit from his decisions, administrators at least assure themselves of effective friends when attacks develop. This form of politics, often more important than contests between parties, involves ties among administrators within the executive branch, Congressmen and Senators, and organized interest groups. Here is a pattern of responsibility even where the President is not actually in control of all the many agencies which are nominally under his command and part of the executive branch of which he is the constitutional head.

Thus there are many ways that bureaucracy is held responsible to the people for its actions. One is the fundamental requirement that actions be based on law, including court decisions, congressional statutes and Constitutional requirements. When the provisions of law become unsatisfactory to the public, there are ways of changing them. A second means lies in the professional competence of the civil servants, their adherence to the objective standards of their professions, whatever specialty they practice. A third is their obedience to their political superiors in the executive establishment, ultimately to the President, the elective head and formal link to the electorate. A fourth is the array of largely informal systems of direct consultation with parts of the public and its representatives. Underlying all these is that the bureaucracy in America is not a special mandarin caste but an open body of public servants from most parts of American society generally sharing the values and tastes of that society.

The role of the presidency is nevertheless critical. While most civil servants can be relied upon to keep within the laws by which their activities are ruled, the existence of a system of hierarchy with clear authority at the top is an important insurance of legal observance. Moreover, reference to law and science cannot actually determine the value choices which must be made if government is to operate; some reference to the public is necessary. This leaves much of the problem to the various systems of informal consultation many agencies have worked out with the groups and individuals most directly involved, or to the President and his own appointees. But between these last two possibilities there are important differences. While the systems of bureaucratic consultation are able to account for the wishes of the groups directly consulted, they are less able to weigh the interests of those who are indirectly affected and those who are less vocal or less informed. Moreover, the individual agencies usually have close associations with the directly affected groups (their "clientele"). The President, on the other hand, is responsible to the whole electorate and can have no peculiar ties to one group. The formal system of bureaucratic responsibility which culminates in his office accordingly has to care for the groups and individuals indirectly affected by the actions of the many bureaus and agencies.

Bureaucratic Responsibility

The magnitude of this presidential responsibility is difficult to picture. The federal government employs approximately two-and-a-half million people; of these approximately 30,000 are in the legislative and judicial branches, the others are in the executive. This horde of people is distributed among a bewildering number of departments, government corporations, agencies, and bureaus. By one count there are something more than 1800 divisions, branches, offices and other subunits in the executive. Few of the specialized skills of modern man are not represented among their activities. Yet this is the establishment which the President must direct and in some sense hold accountable to the people of the United States.

Even if the executive branch were purely patterned after a military model, which it is not, the problem of gaining simple obedience to the President's direction would be enormous. There would not only be simple failures of communication but honest misunderstandings, and on occasion willful confusion and indulgence of cross-purposes. Some goals would be unwittingly assigned to different units and others would be unassigned. Many decisions would be passed on wrong information and some on very nearly none at all. Such difficulties are common in any large organization and at best they can only be minimized, never eliminated. They occur in the federal bureaucracy.

The federal bureaucracy, moreover, has built into it a whole series of obstacles to presidential influence. One of the most important is inertia, a tendency to go on doing what has always been done. It is the consequence not merely of habit and an impulse to "play it safe," but of an endless list of rules and procedures designed for the admirable purpose of eliminating personal whim and preference. This "red tape" genuinely protects citizens against favoritism and corruption but it also implies an established way of doing things and, often, particular policies. This may be well and good as long as the established ways and policies are appropriate, but enormously frustrating when change is attempted.

An essential part of any President's undertaking is to place his own men—men who see things his way and will consult with him on critical questions of policy—in posts of control in the vast bureaucratic mechanism. These men are "political appointees," that is, they are not subject to the normal procedure of selection by competitive examination. It is entirely right that there should be such appointees; these are the men who will decide important policy and be responsible to the President and through him to the American people for the consequences. When in the eyes of the public or of the President they fall short, he can ask for their resignations and replace them. They are usually men with the special quality of sensitivity to public desires and moods that all able politicians must have. But should only department heads and that general category of posts for which the consent of the Senate is necessary be appointed in this way? How can a lonely bureau chief as the only presidential man in the bureau hope to control a functioning organization sufficiently to know what is going on and seize the initiative on matters of policy? How far down the ranks is it necessary to place such appointees?

An administration long in office is tempted to reduce severely the number of such appointees and to establish important policy-determining posts as professional civil service jobs. In this way policies that the incumbent President and his administration are interested in can be placed beyond easy later challenge. The temptation of a new administration and a new President, on the other hand, is to increase the number of political appointees so that direction can more readily be changed. The issue became acute in 1953, when a Republican administration succeeded the Democrats after twenty years during which there had been profound innovations of policy. President Eisenhower had promised a whole new direction of policy, but he found that to take control of the cumbersome bureaucratic behemoth of which he was the nominal head and to turn it in the new direction seemed almost impossible. His increase of the number of posts labeled political ("Schedule C"), brought cries from Democrats that Mr. Eisenhower was undermining the civil service system. The problem of maintaining responsible government he thus attempted to solve was nonetheless real.

Furthermore, the number of men who are both political leaders and sympathetic to the program of an incoming President are not enough to fill all the posts that control the bureaucratic machine. The President will inevitably have to appoint others whom he knows slightly or not at all. He will also have accumulated political debts to political leaders and groups that supported him in his campaign, who may expect certain appointments to go according to their wishes. Even a President in office for some time needs the support of some groups to carry out important projects. Appointments to office—patronage in a sense, but at a high level—are essential devices of the political art. The difficulty is that the ends of bureaucratic control and of acquiring political support are often mutually exclusive. A political appointee to the Department of Agriculture, say, recommended by a large farm organization that has supported the President cannot be readily removed or expected to be simply the President's man in the executive. He is a political officer in his own right, rather as if he had won office by election.

If establishing and maintaining command is difficult, knowing how to use it and for what ends is yet more so. A President is not a specialist, yet he must take action on the basis of the most abstruse information. Gaining the services of the very ablest specialists the nation affords is not a major problem; a call from the President of the United States is very nearly impossible to refuse. But who are the experts and which of them should be called? Next, having selected his experts, what is he to make of their advice? They may disagree. Or they may give advice which for perhaps indefinable reasons arouses his suspicions. He may sense that mixed with the technical judgment are private preferences and biases. Perhaps no more serious recent example of this has occurred than in President Kennedy's decision to approve the adventure at the Bay of Pigs in 1961. The operation had been started before Kennedy came to office; he was presented with the plans before he had opportunity to assess his advisers. The military strongly advised going ahead with the well-advanced undertaking; failure, he was told, was highly unlikely. With some reluctance he assented; the results were disastrous. President Johnson has had his own reasons for mistrusting expert military advice; repeatedly in Vietnam the successes promised from particular forms of escalation have not appeared. Nor is the military field the only area in which experts need be heard with caution.

The Executive Office

The resources of manpower and organizational machinery at the disposal of the President are not large. As we have seen, controlling the military and two-and-a-half million civil servants is itself no small part of his problem. The number of people whom he can know personally is limited; even a President can count on no more than twenty-four hours a day. When he places his own men in key posts, he must expect that with all the good will and loyalty on their part that could be hoped for, their jobs will require them to see things in a perspective different from his. A high official of the Department of the Interior, for example, cannot be effective in his own job and concurrently be able to see how a decision, say, on matters of oil affects national defense and the long-term conduct of foreign relations. Perspectives will differ, properly, and a President may be wise to ask no more of his Interior friend than that he be a genuine advocate of the views of his Department; it will be the President's responsibility to relate such views to other considerations.

For assistance in his own job the President relies upon a handful of men attached to his office who are not specialists matching those found in the Departments and operating agencies. Even here he has to accept limitations. Perhaps the first officer who comes to mind as a potential high-level presidential assistant is the Vice President. Many times have Presidents announced that the Vice President would henceforth have important responsibilities; each time, however, it somehow works out that the Vice President is not as important as promised and the office is still rewarded with mild amusement. The reason primarily is that the Vice President is not simply the President's man. While the Vice President has been elected directly by the people, he is the potential successor to the President. There is latent tension between generations and between a man and his possible heir. Although Vice Presidents have been given important functions not assigned them by the Constitution and can give material help to their chiefs, frustration is almost inevitable while they are in office; certainly Presidents are unlikely to treat them as seconds-in-command.

The cabinet also suffers from the same fundamental handicap that minimizes the office of Vice President: the Constitution assigns the executive power very simply to the President. Some members may be important political figures in their own right and so be effectively entitled to careful hearing from the President. Others are not, however, and may in fact be overshadowed by some of the bureau chiefs nominally under them. Like the Vice President, they are on hand in the consideration of large decisions only on the call of the President. Some Presidents have made effective use of their cabinets and have sought to benefit from the collective wisdom and discussion; others, however, have not troubled to call many cabinet meetings. President Kennedy, for example, had very few meetings of his cabinet. Ultimately the American cabinet has no genuine collective responsibility and has, as one student has put it, only a "symbolic value."

The really effective assistance to the President today is found in the Executive Office of the President. Though by official reckoning this Office accounts for slightly more than 2000 employees, this figure is very deceptive, for it includes the staffs of the Bureau of the Budget, the Office of Emergency Planning, the Executive Mansion and Grounds, and others with all their stenographers, gardeners, and so on. Many of them continue from administration to administration and are no closer to the President than their counterparts in remote divisions of the government. Only a handful of even the 327 listed (in 1965) as part of the White House Office actually carry major responsibilities or work closely with the President.

During the first few years of the New Deal the whirlwind of events about the White House produced a condition approximating institutional apoplexy. One of the most important studies of the administrative system ever undertaken, that of the Brownlow Committee, proclaimed that "the President needs help." Roosevelt generally lacked his own staff and the nation suffered as a consequence. The President was given his help in the form of a group of assistants with (in the words of the Brownlow Committee) "a passion for anonymity." This seemingly small and obvious reform has been vital to the effective operation of the modern presidency.

"The passionate anonyms," as Washington wits promptly dubbed them, have not always been inconspicuous. In the Kennedy administration some of them were very colorful figures indeed, and several went on toward political careers of their own after leaving the White House. Yet, the idea inherent in their posts was that they should be retiring and capable assistants devoted purely to the President.

The danger which this conception sought to avoid materialized during the Eisenhower administration. Sherman Adams, an unusually competent organizer and former governor of New Hampshire, was the leading presidential assistant and in effect a chief of staff within the White House. Consequently much attention was drawn to him and, having no political base other than the President, he was highly vulnerable to attack. When it became possible to smear his reputation, he became a source of embarrassment to the President and had to resign. The wisdom of obscurity in these posts has, accordingly, resulted in the present practice of giving all men in such posts the same title, "Special

Assistant to the President." Their number has varied but it has been less than ten, and organization among them has been, except during the Eisenhower period, informal and flexible. To a degree the assistants have specialized, but each necessarily must deal with problems in a number of very large areas and be ready to take assignments on short notice as crises develop.

The President also has several other assistants with less general assignments. One is his specialist on foreign policy; others deal with military and scientific affairs. In recent years, the foreign policy assistant has been under attack, particularly when McGeorge Bundy held the post, as the operator of a rival to the State Department. The criticism has no doubt been partly captious, but it does point to a serious problem of organizing White House control: if the reins of control are held too tightly, the operating departments may become irresponsible by leaving their jobs to be done in the White House; but if the reins are held too loosely the departments may also be irresponsible for lack of supervision from the President. There is probably no regular pattern of organization which will prove ideal for all Presidents and in all situations. In order to maintain the degree of coordination and capacity for quick action in times of crisis in any one of a multitude of areas, the organization must be flexible and informal. Most of all, it must be attuned to the particular President and his manner of leadership.

This recently regularized provision of a small corps of assistants dedicated to the President may have mitigated the need some Presidents have felt for close alter egos in the White House. The most well known were Colonel E. M. House, an unusually close assistant to President Wilson, and Harry L. Hopkins, who was perhaps equally close to President Franklin Roosevelt in the later years of his administration. House was a Texas politician who helped gain the presidential nomination for Wilson and then became a personal emissary and advisor of the President. Hopkins was a former social worker and administrator who performed in a similar way for Roosevelt. In the eyes of critics these advisors were Svengali figures of sinister and irresponsible power. Certainly any trusted advisor who sees the President of the United States frequently has great power. The fear of these men has been exaggerated since the President after all is responsible for his actions and is entitled to the most devoted assistance he can find. In House and Hopkins the two Presidents certainly found unusually devoted men. The presidency is at times a notoriously lonely post, as any position of great power must be. The more routinized White House establishment of the present day should, however, lessen if not eliminate the need for such highly personal assistants as House and Hopkins.

Important as is the development of a regular White House staff, a change of perhaps greater significance has come in recent decades at the level next below the White House, the other offices grouped into the Executive Office of the President. Though some staffs continue from administration to administration, on the whole they are instruments of presidential control of government and the critical positions are presidential choices. The National Security Council, given the continuing magnitude of military considerations, has been one of the crucial bodies. Established by statute in 1947, its membership includes the Vice President, the Secretary of State, the Director of the Office of Emergency Planning, the Chief of the Central Intelligence Agency, the Chairman of the Joint Chiefs of Staff, as well as the Secretary of Defense, the Secretary of State, and the President. Thus, the Council has some of the characteristics of the cabinet. Although it is a statutory body its function and utility depend on the use the President makes of it. During the Eisenhower era it had a rather formal structure and staff and operated—as the President wished—in a fairly routinized manner. This manner was changed under Kennedy, who had less taste than his predecessor for this degree of depersonalization. Similar variations according to presidential preferences can be expected.

A less conspicuous, but larger, unit of the presidential establishment is the Office of Emergency Planning. It looks after the civilian aspects of mobilization; in wartime its importance would suddenly emerge. The Office of Science and Technology is relatively new, having been created in response to the spectacular Russian successes in the Eisenhower years. It is unlikely to wither or vanish.

The Bureau of the Budget

The largest, and in some ways the most important, part of the executive establishment is the Bureau of the Budget. The Bureau, whose legislative activities were discussed in the last chapter, has thoroughly outgrown any belief that its reason for being consists of simple economy of government expenditure. It is now the President's chief medium for exercising control and maintaining responsibility to the public of the main body of the government. This function is the outcome—which is not yet fully achieved—of years of evolution. One of the landmarks of these years was its transfer in 1939 from the Treasury to the Executive Office of the President. Through the Bureau, the President now has regular machinery for checking on what the many pieces of government that make up the executive branch are doing and for attempting to coordinate their efforts, both with each other and with his own program.

The problem of size is particularly difficult with the Bureau of the Budget, and it points up an inherent problem of the modern presidency. How large an undertaking should it make? How large should its staff be? In recent years the Bureau has had approximately 500 people, certainly not large as federal agencies go. It would seem that a bigger staff might better allow it to check on all the myriad activities of the federal bureaucracy. Too large a Bureau, however, would seriously impair the responsibility and initiative of the operating agencies. Somewhere between a handful of people making only spot checks on the large problems and a large staff duplicating the planning of individual agencies, there is a proper size and function. Finding this optimum, however, is not simple.

Perhaps the measure of the growing influence of the Budget Bureau is its prestige and ability to attract individuals of high caliber from all parts of government. The Bureau does not have control of the great federal machine, and perhaps it should not; nevertheless it is increasingly an invaluable tool for the President in maintaining responsible bureaucracy. He badly needs it.

In one sense the Budget Bureau and the National Security Council (with its staff) represent an institutionalization and depersonalization of the presidency. Both help the President carry out his policies and programs by giving him control over the executive branch he would not otherwise have. Nevertheless they also provide a means by which executive functions might continue even in the absence of the President; they are capable almost of governing on a sort of professionalized policy independent of the directions given by the elections that choose the Presidents. Conceivably a President might become a figurehead and ceremonial figure and the nightmare of bureaucratic irresponsibility would be a reality. It would be hysterical to proclaim this as a present danger, but there is a potential problem here.

A rather different, but also very important, development in the office of the President is the Council of Economic Advisors. Created by the Employment Act of 1946, it is a group of three economists supported by a small staff. As we already noted, this landmark Act was founded on the economic analysis of J. M. Keynes and had as its premise the fundamental obligation of modern government to act to achieve and maintain full employment. The history of the Act and the Council illustrate the proposition that a large innovation of policy is not achieved by simple passage of an Act of Congress. The Act was a monumental achievement and the outcome of a vast effort, but it represented only one of many steps on the long road leading to acceptance of its purposes. The Council was slowly established and even slower in becoming effective. Under Truman it lacked sureness and, above all, lacked reliable access to its single and indispensable constituent, the President. It was more forceful under Eisenhower, but was led by men who had grave misgivings about the doctrine that underlay their commissions. Under Eisenhower, nevertheless, the Council had an important influence, which its successor members tended to deplore as having been responsible for a serious slack in the economy.

With President Kennedy, however, the Council of Economic Advisors came into its own. Its members were selected to begin work even before the new administration took office, and being articulate, able, and aggressive, with a ready listener as their client, they quickly achieved great stature in the government. Whether because of their advice and its following first by Kennedy and then by Johnson, or because of lucky coincidence, the economy performed as predicted when steps based on Keynesian analysis were taken—increased depreciation allowances, a tax cut and others—and unemployment declined dramatically. The resulting prestige of the Council has by now probably established it as a fundamental tool of government in the United States.

The Council of Economic Advisors has provided a notable increase in the President's ability to manage the economy in the largest sense. With sufficient knowledge of current economic data, government action now may contract or expand aggregate demand for goods and services in the nation so as to reduce unemployment, accelerate growth of the economy or control inflation. This action involves changes in rates and kinds of taxation, in the supply of money and credit, and other devices. Although these actions may affect the distribution of wealth within the nation, the primary focus of concern in the Council's advice to the President is the general level of the economy. A President is not of course able to make the economic life of the nation whatever he pleases, but he has a far greater chance of affecting the economy than hitherto.

Considering that Presidents are notoriously held to blame whenever depressions come, this is no inconsiderable gift. The advice given by the Council can be mistaken (as it has been occasionally in the past); the advice may also be ignored (as it also has been on occasion). It depends on how much the Advisors have gained the President's confidence and on his willingness and capacity to heed them. The Advisors must be technically able, of course, but like the presidential assistants they must be in sympathy and rapport with their client. It is overstating the case to say that the Council is the economic ideologist of the administration. This denies the technical expertise that recent members have plainly brought to the Council. But problems of value preferences are inevitably imbedded in the technical problems and members must accordingly be President's men. Yet the rise of the Council has undoubtedly advanced the institutionalization of the presidency.

The Autonomy of Federal Agencies

This listing of the resources at the direct command of the President suggests that his office has achieved, or is about to, an iron control of the federal behemoth. This is very far from the truth; indeed, it is questionable whether the presidency has kept up with the centrifugal tendency of the government. Many parts of the government have a large degree of autonomy within the bureaucratic structure. At the same time, they have frequently become parts of systems of power that include elements of Congress and interest groups outside of government. There are many variants on this pattern and very important differences of degree among the many sub-systems. The important facts for the presidency, however, are that the bureaus and agencies of the federal government often have their own political sources of support and can act independently of presidential wishes. This condition, well known to most Presidents, makes administration a form of politics, one of the most complex and difficult to be found anywhere. In participating, as he must if he is to fulfill his mandate, a President is at a very serious disadvantage.

The most obvious, although not always the most important, illustrations of his problem are the independent regulatory commissions. These bodies are thoroughly anomalous in terms of the classic picture of the separation of powers; indeed, the Brownlow Committee once termed them collectively, "a headless fourth branch of government." Intended to be free of "politics," which meant party politics, they make rules and also act as quasi-judicial bodies. Their membership, once appointed, is presumably free from the presidential pressure of potential removal, and the commissioners typically have overlapping terms. Behind their creation was an idea of purely expert, scientific, and impartial administration, but because they must decide on matters of policy for which science has no answers, they confront a serious problem of responsibility. Moreover, some of their activities plainly affect fundamental presidential programs and policies. Thus, for example, President Johnson's general economic policy had a subdued clash with the policy of the Federal Reserve Board as enunciated by its chairman, William M. Martin, in early 1966. The Board, fearing inflation, raised interest rates, an action within the board's powers but opposed to the President's general economic policy of the time. Since Mr. Martin was very firm in his position, the President had little choice but to put the best face on the situation he could; as the decision to disagree was amicably announced over television by Mr. Martin and President Johnson it was plain that Johnson preferred discretion to valor in a contest he knew he could not win. To ease the inherently difficult problem of coordinating economic policy the members of President Johnson's Economic Advisors and the members of the Board met for regular luncheon meetings. The friendly discussions may help soften the immediate problem's most severe forms, but they cannot really eliminate the problem, for it goes beyond simple communication and personal friendliness or antagonism. Underlying all the verbal differences are differences of economic philosophies and the support of different constituencies.

The President confronts an essentially similar problem with many other agencies, even when he controls the choice of their chiefs. Thus, agencies in the Department of Agriculture, Commerce, and the Interior notoriously have their own "clienteles" (a word that grossly understates the influence held by the groups in question). A President is formally free, given the consent of the Senate, to appoint whomever he pleases as Secretaries of these departments. Ineptly chosen Secretaries, however, may find themselves isolated and frustrated in their own Departments if they attempt programs unpopular with the clienteles of their Departments. Their orders may not be obeyed, delay may become chronic, and they may find themselves attacked by the congressional committees concerned with their fields. Knowing the problem, a President is likely to find men actively supported by important private interest groups and their spokesmen in Congress. By the same token, however, the President will have yielded any hope of simply ordering his supposed subordinates to do his wishes. Other methods—and perhaps other ends—will have to suffice.

The problem that Presidents confront takes many forms. It is rare for an agency simply to defy presidential authority; it has happened, however. The more typical problems relate to coordination of competing or overlapping programs, reorganization of agencies, and establishment of new policies. In all such problems it is tempting to see merely technical problems of efficient administration. Although there are always technicalities of much complexity, the genuine issues are much larger and much more important.

Thus many Presidents have been troubled by the fierce undercover contests between the various agencies of the federal government dealing with water projects. Study groups such as the Hoover Commissions have emphasized the importance of coordination of these agencies, as have virtually all independent experts on water resource management. Time and again, however, in the Missouri basin, in the Red, White and Arkansas River watersheds, and in other areas, coordinated planning and development have proved impossible. The reason is that the issues involve not only the power of the several agencies, but various interests which regard themselves as the peculiar constituents of various agencies and different values, such as flood control versus irrigation, and so on.

The representative character of many agencies has often frustrated attempts to achieve seemingly sensible and obvious reorganization of the many bureaus in the government. The largest such contest came during the New Deal, when President Roosevelt attempted a large-scale reorganization of the executive branch. A major struggle followed. It was precipitated by the resistance of the Forest Service to transfer from the Department of Agriculture—where it had enjoyed autonomy and generally friendly relations with its lumber industry clientele—to the Department of the Interior, where conservation would clearly have been made a stronger objective. Similar fears of disturbed relationships between agencies and their established constituencies in other fields were mobilized, so that when the issue reached Congress, the opposing coalition was formidable and the plan was emasculated. Although most of the discussion related to efficient organization, the genuine issues were much larger.

The problem of establishing a new policy sponsored by the President is equally difficult. Repeatedly, new objectives in fields of federal action already occupied by existing agencies have met great obstacles. Thus when an attempt was made in the 1930's to alleviate rural poverty, it was necessary to create an entirely new agency, the Farm Security Administration (as it ultimately became), although a bureau already existed in the field, the Agricultural Extension Service. The latter, however, had not touched the problem of the rural poor and was supported by various congressmen and the American Farm Bureau Federation and the agricultural colleges; together these constituted a power structure that destroyed the Farm Security Administration and its program. The innovation of policy here had to rely on presidential support, but even this in the end was insufficient. A more recent story is the effort to improve the quality of water and to control pollution. The purpose was confided to the established U.S. Public Health Service, but ultimately it was necessary to create a new agency. The new agency met prompt resistance.

The problem a President confronts as administrator, then, is exceedingly difficult. He cannot simply command. He now has improved means for learning what is going on and for reaching out to the different parts of government for which he cannot escape being held responsible. Nevertheless, he cannot attempt great change without very large effort, and he must tailor his ventures to the total resources of his political power. The administrative part of his task is as political as anything he does. The methods adopted by different Presidents necessarily vary with their personalities and, more important, with their political situations and the number of their objectives. Franklin Roosevelt has often been charged with disorderliness of administration and love of chaos. He frequently allowed different administrative leaders to engage in public combat over which agencies should undertake which jobs for which ends by which methods. In the process he learned a great deal about the distribution of power behind the contenders and consequently often achieved compromises favorable to his own ends. Most Presidents, however, have not had his peculiar gifts and have been unwilling to allow the surfacing of so much conflict within their administrations.

For all that administration seems technical and a matter of purely organizational and managerial skills, it is intensely political for it involves the distribution of benefits and deprivations to different groups and the favoring of some values over others. This is most true at the White House level. Here as elsewhere in his job, the President must be a leader.

Chapter V

PRESIDENTIAL

LEADERSHIP

The more intensively the power of the presidency is analyzed the more elusive it becomes. The formal powers granted by the Constitution are negligible by any strict reading of the actual language, and they are often stalemated by the grants to Congress. The vast machinery of the executive branch, far from being a finely tempered instrument under the President's control, is one of his major problems. Yet the reputation of the office remains one of great power; and the reputation is largely justified. To a remarkable degree this power consists of the opportunities for leadership the office gives.

These opportunities vary enormously, both with the times and with the man who is President. Somewhere mixed in the whole of presidential history is the element of chance, or as Machiavelli put it, Fortune. Presidents who in some circumstances might have risen to genuine greatness never gained the opportunity. Thus, in different circumstances Theodore Roosevelt might have made a decisive mark on history just because of his personal vigor and belief in the strenuous life; as things were, his opportunities were few and his actions were less impressive than the noise accompanying them. As one perhaps malicious observer noted, it was his misfortune not to be a war President. Somewhat similarly, John F. Kennedy came to office with a commitment to vigor and a desire to carry through programs of social reform; his slender majority, the existence of a severe balance of payments problem and his brief time in the presidency left him a record of few achievements. Harry Truman, on the other hand, finding himself abruptly projected into the presidency and at first afflicted with a sense of inadequacy, rose to near greatness. Nevertheless, it remains true that the American presidency holds potentialities that may be grasped, some by any man who manages to reach the office, others only by the strongest and ablest of Presidents. Other than its formal machinery what are the inherent assets of the office?

The Prestige of the President

First, perhaps, is the sheer mystique of the office. The moment the successful candidate has been elected, he becomes a man set apart. His friends cease to address him by his first name and he walks in an atmosphere of deference and awe. His every glance and gesture are noted and searched for meaning. His clothes, his books, his pets, these and other features of his private life become matters of triumph or anguish to vociferous professional spokesmen. His most casual strolls are dogged by eagle-eyed protectors and his daughters have the unflagging chaperonage of agents from the Secret Service. Seemingly everything about him is reported to the public, and nearly everything is criticized. More thoroughly than anyone else he has lost his privacy. It is as though all the exposure, publicity and captious criticism of his personal foibles were intended to remind him that he is mortal and not divine.

The aura of grandeur remains, however; no exposure of pettiness or human fallibility can destroy it. Indeed, the attention that hangs upon his every word and all the criticisms are signs that the President combines the symbolic role of chief of state with that of head of government. Every expectation proclaims that he is a man of power and at every point the expectation is itself a source of power. Since he is believed to be powerful and since he is symbol of the nation itself, he is often heeded for no other reason at all, even when reflection indicates he has no capacity for compulsion. Thus an invitation to the White

House, whether for a conference in an industrial crisis or for a reading of poetry, is very nearly a summons. The invitation may indeed be declined, but the refusal is loaded with political significance.

The endowment of this power comes with the office, but the power itself is limited within obscure and indefinable limits and it can never be used carelessly lest it be diminished. Some Presidents have been able to add to it and others have vastly decreased it. When, for example, a President uses it to gain a settlement of an industrial dispute, he is likely to find (as did President Kennedy) that its force is roughly proportionate to the infrequency with which he applies it. Used in other than rare and exceptional circumstances, it also weakens the ordinary and mundane processes by which such crises are normally settled. Here is a paradox: the prestige of the presidency and the awe it inspires carry power only to the extent it is not used. How then is prestige a source of power?

This question has no easy answer. Partly it is that the prestige of the office carries real though limited power. The limits apply more to frequency of use than to its extent. Moreover, its use requires an almost exquisite sensitivity in the President himself. He must know when to invoke it and when to reserve it. He must also know how to use it. Since much of its force, like magic, lies in its mystery and its uncertain consequences, it is usually best used in combination with other and more explicit power. That is, prestige is genuinely useful up to the point at which it meets an explicit test; such a test may well destroy it.

There has been no more vivid illustration of this than the 1962 steel crisis. In this incident President Kennedy committed his prestige to gain agreement by the industry and union for only moderate increases in prices and wages. His plan called for behavior very different from that of the past. The President and his White House associates felt they had achieved a dramatic success of industrial diplomacy when the union reluctantly agreed to forego the advantages it had in direct negotiations with the industry and settled for a relatively moderate wage increase. So far, the President, largely by making use of the awe inspired by his office, had succeeded. There was a second part of the diplomatic arrangement which the President thought the industry had accepted, however: led by the United States Steel Corporation it would similarly refrain from increasing its prices excessively. United States Steel, however, having accepted the first part of the implied bargain (a low wage settlement), proceeded to raise prices substantially.

At this point, the President's prestige not only failed to solve the specific problem, it reached the brink of its own destruction for future purposes. Unless the President could now manage to force the industry as represented by U.S. Steel to rescind its action, labor would henceforth no longer trust the President and would become more intransigent than ever. The steel industry would also have proved that it had no need to listen to him. Nor would this be the end of the chain of consequences. With the rest of the country and the world watching, others would draw similar conclusions. How far the results might reach would be unforseeable but certainly they might prove dire. The President had taken an enormous gamble, probably without perceiving what the stakes were, and he faced an abyss.

Now fully aware of his peril, President Kennedy went into a whirlwind of activity. Everything that anybody close to him could think of was tried; in substance it was very little, for there were virtually no powers of coercion in his hands. The appearance of activity, however, successfully disguised his impotence for a critical two days. Then by the greatest of ironies it turned out that U.S. Steel had miscalculated on what it should have been most knowing, the state of the market for steel. Just as the White House was shooting its last and noisiest bolts, the weak market forced U.S. Steel to rescind its action. The President was given credit for vast determination and overwhelming power; his prestige rose to new heights. He had, nevertheless, subjected his office, and the country, to grave peril.

President Eisenhower was cautious and sparing in the use of his prestige. He took great care not to spend it, even under intense provocation. Yet this policy in its way was as dangerous as President Kennedy's recklessness in the steel crisis. A dramatic illustration is Eisenhower's conduct during Senator McCarthy's attack on the Army. When Secretary of the Army Stevens was subjected to humiliating treatment by the Senator, a series of strong statements of support for the Secretary from the President could have done much to protect him. The support was minimal, the President preferring to stay above the battle and to protect the dignity of his office. Many concluded that, whether the President could not or merely would not expend his resources for his own subordinates, he could not be relied upon, and that they should protect themselves as best they could. This widespread conclusion resulted in a serious deterioration of the quality of government. Excessive protection of prestige can also be a mistake.

To separate out presidential prestige in this manner, however, is misleading. Although prestige is a component of power, it is really less a source than an aspect of power. The power of the President is very much like his functions. Thus it has been fashionable to discuss the various roles of the President and indeed it is often useful to do so. Nevertheless, a President seldom can be expected to think of himself as performing now this role, now that, and now another. They mingle and affect one another to such a degree that they are actually indistinguishable. During the course of almost any day, he moves from meetings with his subordinates dealing with complex problems of organization to ceremonial functions of dedicating monuments to welcoming ambassadors to signing of bills—without break or clear transition.

Thus, the formal interview at which the President first greets a newly arrived ambassador may color the interpretive reports which that ambassador sends his government when serious matters impend. Is the President of the United States a man of great shrewdness? Can he be expected to behave with force, or will he be likely to vacillate in crisis? Similarly, the manner and authority with which a President responds to questioning in a press conference will bear on the course of legislation before Congress, on the zeal with which officers in various departments pursue particular programs, on the estimates which the electorate makes of him. So also with his speeches; they seldom can be expected to sway many by their sheer logic or eloquence, yet they leave a residue of impressions. Is the President devious? is he a man of character? are questions in the minds of most of his hearers, no matter what the subject matter of his speeches. No one speech or one interview or ceremonial act will have a decisive effect on presidential power or the course of events, but collectively all of them affect the outcome of large affairs.

If presidential conduct of even the seemingly most empty and formal parts of his office is important, it does not follow that the importance consists of winning great popularity. It is quite possible to be popular simply by not giving offense. To a great extent this was President Eisenhower's course, and in his time it had merit. Nevertheless, popularity achieved at the expense of action is usually a renunciation and a negation of power. A policy of attempting to please everyone, moreover, will probably end in pleasing no one; popularity is not the same as power and may often be incompatible with it.

Mobilizing His Support

The point at which presidential popularity and power meet is the hold of the President on his own constituency. Whenever he is able to mobilize even a substantial part of it, he is a truly formidable figure. Achieving this at any time other than national crisis is extraordinarily difficult. The general public—his constituency—is normally ill informed and apathetic even when issues of the greatest moment are at stake. While any President can command some attention to almost any topic with which he is concerned, the task is more difficult for some Presidents than for others, and the degree of support that can be obtained varies greatly. It is at just this point, of obtaining a hearing, that presidential popularity and style are important. Although Franklin Roosevelt had popular support for his program as strong as any President has enjoyed, he nonetheless had to overcome well-entrenched opposition in Congress to many of his objectives. He accordingly inaugurated the practice of speaking directly to the public by radio. His voice was golden and the appeal of his personality came through the static; his appeals were frequently successful. When President Kennedy encountered similar congressional opposition and was urged to use Roosevelt's "fireside chat" device, he pointed out that already he had used it as often as his predecessor. Strangely, everyone recalled the performances of FDR as having been much more frequent than in fact they had been. President Kennedy was correct, not only in his count, but in his refusal to appeal to the public by television too frequently. During his first year in office, President Johnson discovered that he was in danger of "overexposure." He curtailed his television appearances lest this particular form of political currency be hopelessly debased (and television audiences become too angry over the displacement of favorite programs).

Although a President can generate mass support across the nation for some particular end, he may yet fail to achieve that end simply because the support is weak in a particular area, say, one electing the man who happens to be chairman of a crucial congressional committee. Overwhelming support in New York and California for a presidential program may thus count for little if the President's program must be reported out by the House Interior Committee and that committee is headed by a hostile congressman from western Colorado. There may indeed be things that the President can do to move the congressman, but these will not include the President's public appeal.

Much of the time, then, the President must rely on techniques other than his ability to speak to the nation. He will have to behave like other politicians(or statesmen): bargain and negotiate. This necessity follows particularly from the fact that political power in the United States is on the whole locally based. This means that the President must deal with key congressmen and senators. Here, an intimate knowledge of the way Congress operates and of the particular needs of its individual members is extremely valuable. President Johnson has probably exhibited his greatest skill here. President Kennedy, also an ex-senator, was informed, but he lacked the long years of congressional experience and the special flair his successor has. President Eisenhower, on the other hand, lacked the experience of either Kennedy or Johnson; in part because of this the presidency in his time was very different than under his successors.

Bargaining and negotiating are the very essence of most administration also. In the choice of high-level bureaucrats they involve not only the particular agencies but senators and congressmen and interest group leaders as well. In the conflicts among rival agencies that are such a recurrent feature of American government the President can rarely order conflict stopped, since the issues are almost always policy matters that affect the interests of divergent groups in the general population. Often the best that a President can hope to do is to mediate, and this frequently proves futile. Sometimes a President finds himself inescapably drawn into contests between management and labor, as in those in steel. He may summon the parties to the White House, offer the services of government mediators, and lay on the pressure of public opinion. This aspect of the President's task is sometimes included under "the power to persuade," but simple presentation of rational arguments is seldom sufficient.

The different problems and skills involved in these various modes of politics account for the "styles" of various Presidents quite as much as differences in personality. Understandably, a President such as Lyndon Johnson, who rose to prominence by his success in negotiation in Congress, is likely to rely on such methods when he reaches the White House; just as understandably Woodrow Wilson or John Kennedy, who both had relied on strong moral appeals to the general public, would be expected to seek to make their mark by mobilizing their own large constituency. And a President such as Dwight Eisenhower, who was primarily concerned with the prestige and dignity of his office, will be tempted to remain apart from the hurly-burly of political conflict.

The heavy reliance on one or another of these political styles, however, may or may not be appropriate to the problems of the times. It is doubtful whether the moralism of Woodrow Wilson was the most valuable approach to the greatest problem of his time: achieving a sane international settlement after World War I. His vision of the League of Nations as a broad moral concern of the peoples of the world did leave an important legacy, which had a continuing effect in later years, but his cause might have been better served if he had counseled and bargained more intimately with the United States Senate. President Kennedy had a keen awareness of his need for congressional support, but he lacked the special talent to gain it that Lyndon Johnson brought to the presidency. By the same token, however, Johnson suffered from an inability to project a sense of moral cause to the general public. Perhaps President Eisenhower, at least in the early years of his administration, was in the happiest of circumstance of offering a style that met the primary need of the time. As Walter Lippmann observed, Eisenhower was a "healing President"; by simply doing little himself and exuding calm and dignity, he helped to restore a temper of reason to a political scene overheated by increasingly violent charges and countercharges.

The President's task does not permit a choice among these modes. Any President must use all of them, however much his own personal proclivities incline him toward one or another. There are occasions when a President must speak to the nation, others when he must bargain with congressmen and private citizens, and still others when he must put on a regal air. Generally, to the degree a President seeks to influence the long-term future and bring about profound reform he must appeal to the great constituency of the nation at large; to the degree he seeks immediate action he must negotiate with the power holders of the moment; and to the degree he seeks stability and peace he must place himself above the tumult of the time.

As much as anything else this is why the American presidency is so very nearly an impossible job: the various requirements of personality are not necessarily incompatible, but their appearing together in just the right proportions in any individual is inevitably rare. Perhaps the best hope is that the voters will have an intuitive sense of the primary needs of the time and choose the man whose personality and training emphasize the style appropriate to the most important of those needs.

Decisions and Alternatives

The greatest barrier to understanding the presidency today is a widespread misconception of the character of modern government. By this view, government makes decisions, and chooses among clear alternatives with foreseeable results. "Decision-making" has become a term in high intellectual fashion. In some respects, the emphasis on decisions has great merit; it draws attention to real events and escapes from airy abstractions beyond empirical testing. At its best, the approach seeks to identify all the varied participants and influences that go into the *process* of decision-making.

This emphasis, however, creates an illusion of a more rational and less complex world than in fact exists. What may appear from a distance to be a "decision," that is, a deliberate choice between clearly understood alternatives made by thoughtful individuals, on closer examination may turn out to be nothing of the kind, but instead something much more nearly approximating an accident. The participants in the "decision" may be more numerous than appear from outside. The considerations involved almost invariably are more complex than can be seen by outsiders. What actually moves the participants in the decision may not be what should have been considered; and what appear as alternative choices may on close examination not be alternatives at all. Finally, the consequences of the "decision" may be utterly different from those intended; on occasion they are intended but result from forces very different from those invoked.

These complexities are probably easiest to see in the legislative process. Here the number of participants is apparent, as are all the varied influences that affect the outcomes of congressional votes: the pleadings of lobbyists, constituents' letters to congressmen, the President's speeches, the chance events that appear in newspaper headlines, and so on. In the Supreme Court, which issues decisions—officially called that—the complexity of the decision process is often visible. The presidency, however, is held by a single individual who gives orders that seem to be the outcome of his own personal weighing of crisply presented alternatives whose probable consequences are indicated by an efficient staff. If rationality in this sense of decision-making is to be found anywhere, it should be at the apex of the government machine, the presidency.

It is true that the President makes decisions. He signs—or vetoes—

bills before they become law. He chooses men to staff the chief offices of the administration. He sends messages and recommendations to Congress. Yet these are formal actions, and often these "decisions" are largely rituals. Many of the seemingly clear-cut decisions of the President, moreover, are much less obviously clear from the White House perspective at the time they are taken. Thus, one of the most incisive choices made by a President in recent history was Kennedy's action in the Cuban missile crisis. In retrospect it seems to have been a really dramatic turning point in modern times. The crisis appeared at the time (and still seems so) to have been a moment when mistaken action could have plunged the world in destruction. By some accounts President Kennedy's was an incisive choice among a limited group of "options"; he made the correct one and history was tranformed. Later accounts, however, indicate that the action was tentative and uncertain, and that later actions were planned in a pattern of gradual escalation in a situation whose evolution was utterly unforeseeable. Much of the story is still obscure, since little is known of events and understandings in Moscow. Even in this very dramatic confrontation the retrospectively perceived pattern of "crisis—decision—intended outcome" is misleading; the reality through which the major participants, including the President, lived was much more complex.

This decision, like many others, recalls the battle of Borodino described by Tolstoy in *War and Peace:* contact broken between parts of the battlefield, messages lost, delayed or misunderstood, generals issuing irrelevant orders on the basis of mistaken understandings of the reality about them.

The genuine choices of political leaders are apt to be small ones. This is not to say that the choices are unimportant. Much that is later regarded as the result of some "great decision" is actually the consequence of a multitude of lesser decisions taken for reasons not seen as bearing on the ultimate events which they determine. To take another seemingly incisive (and as it proved, mistaken) presidential choice, President Truman's decision to seize the steel mills in 1952; the action was actually the outcome of a long sequence of actions and events that stretched back in time for several years. These included passage of the Taft-Hartley Act in 1947, the ambiguity of a critical piece of subsequent legislation, the vague but real concession to labor leaders given by the government to persuade them to participate in the Wage Stabilization Board in 1951, the silence of industry leaders about the strength of their anger over the government's concessions to labor, the acceptance by union leaders of a presidential plea to delay a strike, the unintended agreement of a rattled government lawyer to a suspicious judge's suggestion that the President was laying claim to "unlimited power"—these incidents were components of a "decision" that was not intended until almost the moment it occurred.

Many actions by national leaders are of this nature. It is rather as though a band of travelers were headed down a road whose end they could neither see nor know. They come to a fork in the way and arguments are propounded for one choice or the other and ultimately one is chosen. The party continues in the general direction it had originally intended, but perhaps the chosen fork later curves slightly; the ultimate end is changed. More important, the possibilities once offered in the choice rejected have probably been foreclosed, since on this journey it is not often possible to turn back and try again. Since there are many such forks and many such unwitting rejections of latent possibilities, often the great acts that seem to be the results of rational decisions are more nearly the inescapable outcomes of previous history.

The President seems to have a freer hand in foreign affairs than elsewhere. He is inevitably *the* authoritative spokesman of the United States in confrontation with other nations. He is not checked by political sub-systems of power and influence as he is in domestic affairs. There are interest groups that intervene in some questions of foreign policy, but they are less pervasive than in other areas. The presumption of a national interest in foreign affairs, moreover, is stronger. The Constitution gives Congress the power to declare war and the Senate power to pass on major diplomatic appointments and treaties, but even here a President has great advantages over Congress. By his actions he can make war very nearly inevitable, and produce a situation in which Congress has no choice other than to make the formal declaration; but even this formality can be avoided. The last two major conflicts of the United States, Korea and Vietnam, both large scale by any test other than that of the two World Wars, were fought without a constitutional declaration by Congress.

Decisions in foreign affairs, however, are often more complex than they at first appear. The decision to intervene in Vietnam is one of the most fateful of recent times; it would seem a vital case of presidential decision-making. Yet which President made the decision? The answer is not clear. President Eisenhower refused large military intervention to save the French when they were faced with disaster at Dien Bien Phu in 1954, but in 1955 he approved American help in training South Vietnam's army, and in 1957 Americans were wounded in Vietnam. In 1961 President Kennedy increased the number of U.S. military advisers to the South Vietnamese forces. In 1964, after American naval ships were attacked in the Gulf of Tonkin, President Johnson sought and got from Congress a resolution giving him authority to resist aggression in Southeast Asia; American troop strength increased to 25,000. In 1965 continuous bombing of North Vietnam began; the increase of troops accelerated.

In time it will be possible to look back and see which of these steps were the most important. Historians will be able to suggest that actions other than those taken at particular moments were possible and that *the* decision was made by a particular President; it is nevertheless probable that the President did not see matters in the historian's clear light when he made the decision.

There are also limitations on presidential choices in foreign affairs imposed by public opinion. Thus in 1945 and 1946 public pressure to "bring the boys back home" and to demobilize the armed forces was irresistible, despite the strong diplomatic reasons for maintaining a strong force in Europe. Walter Lippmann once despairingly asserted that the public has a propensity for being wrong on the important questions of foreign policy since its opinion is always based on situations not of the present but of the past. Public opinion, he argued, is always against any change of policy: if the nation is at peace but becomes threatened, the public refuses to support a war; once war has been declared, the public is against making peace when the opportunity arises. This pessimistic picture is undoubtedly overdrawn. It does underline a genuine difficulty, however; much of the work of diplomacy and the management of foreign affairs must be conducted quietly and out of sight, and it is impossible in the nature of things for the public to be fully aware of the realities and the possibilities, and the dangers.

The enormous complexity of "decision-making" in the White House has far-reaching implications for presidential leadership. The first of these is that the President cannot be regarded as a generalissimo issuing commands and seeing them obeyed. It was put bluntly in Truman's famous remark that Mr. Eisenhower on coming to the presidency would give orders and nothing would happen. While the giving of orders is often part of a President's task, it is only a part and not the most essential; indeed it may sometimes be that when he gives orders he betrays his own failure. Beyond this, leadership in the presidency is not actually a matter of parts at all; it is more realistically the total performance of the President and his office. And this includes his bearing in ceremonies, his dignity and calm under stress, and a host of other intangibles.

A major part of presidential leadership occurs before the time of crisis. The actions taken in a crisis such as that of the missiles in Cuba or the confrontation between President Kennedy and Roger Blough of U.S. Steel undoubtedly receive greater public attention. Their success or failure, however, heavily depend on the degree to which the President has succeeded in establishing the confidence of the general public and of his own associates and subordinates; they also depend on the estimate of himself that his previous actions have created in the minds of his opponents. Thus it is probable that President Kennedy's previous handling of a minor issue involving Blough affected the latter's estimate of the President. In 1961 Blough was Chairman of the Business Advisory Council, a body of leading businessmen attached to government yet private. Secretary of Commerce Luther Hodges sought to correct those of its practices that seemed questionable; the Council tacitly defied Hodges and withdrew from its association with his Department. President Kennedy, in an apparent effort to placate organized business, gave the Council's action his blessing, but in doing so undermined Hodges' position and opened himself to the assessment that he would give way under pressure. This background suggested Kennedy would probably accept a *fait accompli* in the steel price increase. If this was true, the earlier yielding helped bring on the later crisis. At the same time, however, President Kennedy had succeeded by his general conduct of his office in holding the various parts of government together so that in the crisis he was able to create an illusion of massively organized government power arrayed against U.S. Steel. His luck did the rest. Similarly in the Cuban missile crisis, Kennedy's past actions (as in the confrontation in steel for example) helped to form the expectation of American willingness to take drastic action, an expectation that induced Khrushchev to withdraw the missiles. But by the same token, if the Russian leader had not had an earlier very different expectation, one drawn from the impression given by Mr. Kennedy during the celebrated meeting between the two men in Vienna, perhaps the rash Russian attempt would never have been made.

The Character of the President

If the President's problem is as large and diffuse as these events suggest, the personal characteristics he need bring to the office are exceedingly difficult to define. It is easy to say that he should have *charisma,* the God-given quality of the "born leader." About this, however, there is little to say other than to name it, and to note that it is a quality possessed by surprisingly few American Presidents. Of modern Presidents it will probably be agreed that Franklin and Theodore Roosevelt were natural leaders. In the presence of his still proliferating myth, President Kennedy remains a question on this score; it is nevertheless possible that he in fact lacked the quality. There are no others among twentieth-century Presidents, and few among their predecessors, who could be labeled charismatic, yet they included many highly successful leaders.

If the gifted natural leader behind whom men will instinctively fall in line has been rare among American Presidents, there are probably reasons that lie deep in American character and American politics. Americans have generally distrusted men strikingly endowed with the "charismatic" quality. The egalitarian spirit of American life noted by observers of the United States from Tocqueville on sooner or later produces a widespread inclination to diminish the stature and reputation of any man who becomes eminent. Adulation of leaders does occur, but most commonly and most strongly after they are dead. Beyond this, the political institutions of the nation place many barriers in the way of anyone who might remotely suggest a man on horseback. Power to operate through these institutions must surmount innumerable local and functional obstacles not easily passed without negotiation and payment of tribute; to brush them aside would require a mass movement of dimensions and intensity unlike anything seen in America.

The inborn qualities that give success in presidential leadership are thus rather different from those that first come to mind at mention of "natural" leadership. The most obvious is the highly intuitive capacity to sense the state of public feeling—to assess the extent and intensity of satisfaction, dissatisfaction, and even the *potential* pleasure or displeasure of the nation as a whole and as a collection of factions. Experience, study, and training undoubtedly deepen this capacity, but ultimately it is a natural gift that a successful President must have. Whatever the resources of attitude and opinion surveys placed at his disposal, the President must test them by his own intuition and interpret them. This is not to say that presidential leadership is a trick by which a President, having sensed the state of the public mind, scurries to assume a position perfectly attuned with it. He must make his assessment of existing opinion, but he must also lead. Franklin Roosevelt gave a splendid example of what is involved when he made his famous "Quarantine Speech" in 1937 warning of the Nazi danger. He was clearly ahead of public opinion and he quickly realized that he was in danger of becoming isolated in the van. He retreated, but only sufficiently to renew contact with those he had to lead.

The ability to negotiate and bargain among significant and coherent segments of the political public is also related to inborn traits of personality. This ability is shared by many individuals who have no potential for leadership, but the charm, cool-headedness, and other qualities that yield success in mediation—or even selling—are highly useful in the higgling which goes on in the political market place, a process from which no President who wishes to influence the course of things can be aloof. Perhaps to say this is to degrade the concept of leadership to something less exalted than many would wish. Nevertheless, even when the process is scorned as so much "wheeling and dealing," the results obtained are frequently as acceptable as those won by more glorious battles.

There is also usually something intensely personal, whether inborn or not, in the capacity to manage a complex organization. Obviously the talent for administration may be cultivated and improved. Some Presidents, Franklin Roosevelt for example, had neither talent nor taste in this direction. Others, Herbert Hoover most notably, had both the talent and the taste. The ability is certainly valuable in a President, but as the examples chosen suggest, it is far less important than others. It seems almost that purely organizational ability conflicts with political ability, and that to the degree that a President devotes himself to administrative tidiness, he falls short in the more fundamental aspects of his task. Perhaps this underlines the observation that a President must be first of all a politician if he is to be a leader.

The trait that may be ultimately the most important in a President is a sense for power. He must have an almost instinctive understanding of power's sources, its location, and how it may be grasped. Usually this implies that he has a taste for power, although it is not a requirement or even an invariable accompaniment of the sense. It is nevertheless a first essential that a President give unremitting attention to the implications for his power of his every act and, indeed, of virtually everything that happens. It is a paradox that if a President consistently conserves and protects his power he will less frequently be compelled to resort to its overt invocation and application. To cite a famous example, during 1957 President Eisenhower found himself in a situation in which he had no choice but to send a military force into Little Rock after he had created the incorrect impression that he would not act decisively if school integration were opposed. The weakness he seemed to betray became a reality in that greater force than he or anyone else desired became necessary. The simple preference for persuasive and peaceful leadership may sometimes be self-defeating. As in the Little Rock example, the absence of choice even when, or particularly when, the choice left open involves force that he can actually command is a mark of weakness rather than power. Power is greatest and most successful when its overt employment is unnecessary. To achieve this condition, however, a President must always look to the future and to the consequences for his power of his actions. The prospect of a diminution of his power in future crises more than anything else was the main reason for the explosiveness of President Kennedy's reaction to the unexpected announcement of U.S. Steel that its prices were being increased.

However obvious it may be, high intelligence is a primary need in the presidency. Perhaps not everyone would agree that all American Presidents have possessed this attribute, yet most have. Only a few have been men of high culture, but culture is not the same as intelligence. It is more important for a President to possess a common touch than to be at home among the great works of art and literature. Nevertheless, he must be able to gain the services of intellectuals and use their advice. The alienation of the intellectual community from the Republican party during the early Eisenhower years will prove a serious handicap to future Republican Presidents unless it can be repaired. The capacity to grasp the essentials of complex matters, however, is the important intellectual trait of a modern President. When he must decide on costly weapon systems complicated beyond the understanding of any but trained imaginations, when he must weigh the relative costs (political as well as economic) of a seriously adverse balance of payments against a high unemployment, when he must assess the chances for a negotiated peace in a war when a substantial public is rigidly committed to complete victory, when he must do these and many other things concurrently and then mobilize support for his choices, it is obvious that the intellectual demands are hardly less than superhuman.

Vital as these components of presidential leadership are, however, they pale beside an intangible that is virtually immune to analysis—character. In the harsh light of publicity that envelops the presidency, few defects can remain invisible for long. The false and the insincere are likely to be detected by even the humblest watcher on television. It may not occur immediately, but so often is the behavior and the person of the President placed before the public that dissimulation and disguise have little long-term hope. Few men who reach the presidency can expect to be loved or even liked; fortunately, this is not required. It is essential that at crucial moments the President is trusted.

The leadership that the nation must find in its Presidents, then, is not the sort out of which dictators or Caesars are made. The office does not have powers that can be seized to serve the ends of paranoia. Its powers have in a very real sense to be renewed each month and, sometimes, each day. What they are to a very large degree depends upon the quality of presidential leadership. The quality is dependent upon the man who is President, but if the leadership is to succeed it must be accepted by those who follow.

Chapter VI

THE PRESIDENCY IN
THE POLITICAL ORDER

One of the most difficult problems in understanding political reality is the relation between the system's formal and informal aspects. Indeed, it is easy to draw two separate and entirely different pictures, and label one false and the other true. To do this, however, is mistaken. The formal rules set forth in the Constitution and their interpretations by the Supreme Court are hard realities to which practice must conform. The manner of conforming, nevertheless, is often different from anything foreseen by the founders or deducible from the legal documents. The American political order, moreover, while one of the most stable of modern times, is subject to continual change. An accurate description for one era may be quite misleading if applied to another. An account of the political order must be founded on a sense of where it is tending as well as where it has been. The fashionable contrast between modern and traditional societies is never polar; even the traditional societies change, and modern societies—of which the United States is the prime example—have their strong and persistent traditions.

The political system of the United States institutionalizes a variety of values, some of them at odds with each other. An emphasis upon one part of the order emphasizes certain values, and is open to challenge based upon preference for other values. Nevertheless, some values are higher in the general scale of preferences held by the nation at large, and these preferences ultimately test the system and its parts. Evaluation of a particular institution is not merely a matter of taste.

The problem of value preferences is involved in evaluating the presidency. The formal definition of the office is the least complete in the Constitution. It has changed markedly over time and can be expected to change more, even from incumbent to incumbent. And it has often embodied values different from those championed by Congress. It cannot help being caught up in the major currents that sweep American society. And in turn it has enormous capacities for directing those currents. To ask what is to become of the presidency is to ask what is to become of the entire American political order.

Federalism and the Presidency

Americans persistently perceive their government in the terms chosen by the framers of the United States Constitution. There is a great good fortune in this, since the pervasive spirit of the framers' outlook was an emphasis upon liberty. The American reverence for the framers and their work has nevertheless kept alive a vision of politics in the United States that is more and more unrealistic with each year that passes. Constitutional origins and tradition alike dwell upon federalism and the separation of powers. Both doctrines are undeniably woven into the entire system. The difficulty we encounter with them is that neither has had a constant meaning.

The traditional vision is that under federalism government in the United States consists of distinct state and national "levels," each with its own peculiar powers and sources of authority. These two "levels" of government occasionally conflict with each other, raising problems of according to each what is properly its own. For the rest, however, the two go their separate ways performing their separate and characteristic functions. The observations that reality is not quite like this tend to be framed as warnings that corruption or usurpation is taking place, that the federal government is growing strong at the expense of the states.

Such a vision today is unsatisfactory. It is doubtful whether it was ever satisfactory. Shortly after the new government was launched, cries arose to insist that the Constitution was being perverted. Indeed, if we recall the Alien and Sedition Acts, the cries had a foundation that many of their present counterparts lack. Today, however, the picture is not only grossly inaccurate; it is a travesty upon the flexibility of the Constitution drawn in 1787. Federalism in the twentieth century is an intricate pattern of shared functions, the states and the federal government being enmeshed with each other at the inception, the planning, and the execution of many policies. Repeatedly the "central government" is found responding to the initiative of local governments (themselves formally creatures of the state governments), and providing money to the states to be spent by the local units. The process is described nowhere in the Constitution, yet it is thoroughly constitutional. Again and again the supposedly insulated "levels" of government work together so intimately and cooperatively that there seems to be a single coherent system. Yet just as it begins to appear that this, rather than the traditional vision of opposing "levels," is the essential picture, crises involving states' rights and civil rights arise, and it is apparent that reality is very mixed. The truth is that the states have neither been absorbed by nor have absorbed the federal government and that important frictions remain within a system still constantly changing.

Similarly, the traditional vision holds with regard to the separation of powers. The three "coordinate" departments of the federal government, like the two "levels," occasionally clash, but for the most part they also go their separate ways playing their allotted roles. While the conflicts provide drama and receive much attention, the important political reality is the collaboration between the executive and the legislative branches. There are serious conflicts in the making of policy; much of politics has to do with conflict, but many of the most important conflicts occur in *both* branches. The typical pattern, indeed, is one in which some members of the executive and some members of Congress are aligned against other members of the executive and other members of Congress, each side with its supporters in private interest groups and local elites. But so far as the two branches themselves are concerned, the important fact is mutual dependency. Congress is probably increasingly incapable of formulating policy on most of the matters on which it must take formal action. It may alter and criticize proposals before it; often it must mediate the final stages of conflict aroused by the proposals; but only rarely can it successfully introduce and effectuate a major change of policy by its own unaided initiative.

To understand the presidency it is necessary then to look upon the whole system. And in particular it is essential to consider the central problems it has had to solve. The first of these easily tends to be ignored, for it has been solved brilliantly in America. It is, very simply, the problem of unity, of maintaining a single nation. The problem was implicit in the motivation of the remarkable band of men who engineered a virtual *coup d'état* in discarding the Articles of Confederation and substituting the Constitution. It was an issue that smoldered below the surface until 1860, when it brought civil war. Since then, we have tended to take as thoroughly settled that there should be a single nation stretching across a continental expanse and encompassing millions of people from different races, religions, and cultures.

Mere national survival, however, has never been the whole of the American political problem. Survival has always been taken to mean something considerably more, the persistence of values for which the overworked words, equality and liberty, are still the only terms to use. The nation might have continued in being without the ordeal of civil war if the north had been willing to acquiesce in extension of slavery to the West. To achieve aims of liberty and equality concurrently with unity has been enormously difficult.

Federalism has probably been the single most important political device by which the nation has been preserved. This basic compromise has made many others possible. The irony here is that the compromise was between the various states on one hand and the nation on the other, not the most important issue of American history. In a larger sense, however, federalism from the start has been a compromise between the nation and its parts, the parts being not states but less formal units, local and functional elites. Federalism has been the means by which the power held by these groups has been recognized and accepted in return for their acceptance and support of the nation. The fundamental principle underlying this compromise—seen with some clarity by James Madison when the Constitution was formulated—is that small units, being usually less diverse than large ones, are more likely than the large to encourage the structuring of power relationships and the formation of stable elites. Thus state units have not only preserved the power of local elites and interest groups, but have also been the channel for additional resources from the nation to the local units. The nation in return has enjoyed the benefits of the organization and disciplining of elements of the population that might otherwise have gone their separate ways or been disruptive.

The presidency has probably been essential to the success of federalism in the United States. It is, indeed, possible to imagine a United States existing within the framework of the Articles of Confederation, but the absence of a central executive would have condemned such a nation to a much lesser stature. It would have had a poorer economy and a lesser capacity to defend itself; it would have also had many other deficiencies. The character of the executive has been almost as important as the fact of an executive's existence. As we have seen, there was a genuine possibility that a plural or a collegial executive might have been chosen by the constitutional founders. While it might indeed have worked, it is unlikely the nation would have been as cohesive as it has. The nation would have been without an important symbol: even a modern people must have ceremony and ritual if it is to endure the ordeals that accompany common life. More important however, the nation would have sacrificed incisive leadership at critical junctures. If a collegial executive had been adopted by the framers, it might have been chosen either in Congress or directly by the electorate. Either way divided leadership in time of crisis would have been probable. Britain, indeed, has selected her national leaders from Parliament and has been very successful, but she is far less diverse than the United States and in recent times has relied upon party machinery to elevate the leaders above Parliament.

The presidency in representing the national aspect of political life, then, has been important to the evolution of federalism; the office has been the medium for reasserting national values. These values include not only elementary national survival and unity but liberty and equality, which lie at the heart of the American ethos. Repeatedly, the presidency has of necessity been the focus of efforts on behalf of weak minorities and the underprivileged; in recent years it has shared this burden with the Supreme Court. Most of the government initiative to end racial segregation has come from the President and from the Court. When the court decided in 1954 that segregated education was contrary to the "equal protection of the laws" clause of the Fourteenth Amendment, it started a long chain of events. Though state and local governments and individual congressmen could and did resist desegregation, the President and the federal executive were compelled to align themselves with the Court. Even President Eisenhower, who strongly believed in the sanctity of state and local autonomy, responded to defiance in Arkansas with military force.

The reason for the alignment of Supreme Court and the presidency is that both have the same constituency, the whole nation. Both are responsible to *all* the people and neither is susceptible to the pressures of the local holders of power to the degree congressmen and state officials are. This is not to say that either the President or the Court can always be relied upon to defend the rights and interests of the weak, merely that they are better able and hence more likely to do so. Nor can it be assumed that the President and the Court will always take the same view of every controversy. There are different ways of regarding the interests of the weak and not all issues involve such problems. Thus, in the *Youngstown* decision of 1952, the Court resoundingly denied presidential power to seize the steel mills. Thus also the Court very nearly demolished Franklin Roosevelt's New Deal program in a series of adverse decisions. On the whole, however, the Court has been unwilling to oppose presidential power and has avoided doing so whenever it could. The outcome of the Court's demolition activities in the 1930's included the abortive "court packing" incident and then a reversal of the Court's attitude toward New Deal activism; from 1936 on the Court tended to accept programs under legislation sponsored by the President. The hostility of the Court to presidential programs of the early thirties is not likely to be repeated. Some differences and even clashes between the presidency and the Court will occur, but no persistent pattern of hostility is probable.

By contrast with the presidency (and the Supreme Court), the states are necessarily narrow in outlook, and have no forum other than Congress in which anything approaching a view of the nation as a whole is possible. And Congress, being an assembly of the representatives of relatively small constituencies, is able only seldom to rise above the context of the contending claims of these constituencies. Certainly many individual senators and congressmen are men of broad vision, but they have to keep in mind the nature of their own constituencies. Often we like to assume that since all localities of the nation are represented in Congress, all values cherished by the American people are likewise fully represented and that in aggregate Congress represents the nation as well as the President does. This assumption, however, is not justified;

many values and interests are underrepresented or not represented at all in Congress, the interests of the poor and the weak, non-material and aesthetic values especially. In Congress policy tends to be settled by logrolling, by mutual exchange of support among the representatives of different constituencies for their own enterprises, with the result that the interests of groups lacking substantial bases of power in the localities are left out. Just because the President is not selected on this basis and because his responsibility is to all the people, he is able to include in the policies he supports a greater range of interests. His policies as a consequence are more likely to embrace the interests of those who have been left out of the pattern of congressional initiative. The evidence is abundant that if innovations of policy in favor of the poor, of the Negroes, of impotent minorities of all kinds, are to be made, the initiative has to come not only from the executive branch of the federal government, but from the presidency itself. Only the President has the resources of power to act on their behalf, and only he has a constituency constructed so as to include them in the effective scheme of power.

The relationship of the presidency to the basic value of liberty is more complex, but the same set of considerations apply. Since the presidency is the point on which the greatest diversity of pressures come to bear, here the checking of organized power by organized power that Madison noted as the great advantage of a large constituency is at a maximum in the American system. This advantage largely accounts for the ability of the President to initiate programs for the groups at the lower end of the social spectrum. The most vivid modern illustration of this principle in operation is civil rights. Since political power in Mississippi is concentrated in white hands, devolution to the counties of that state or to its governor (or deference to the state's representatives in Congress) necessarily results in perpetuation of the local system in which Negro rights are often ignored. The defense of the rights of Negroes in Mississippi, thus, almost necessarily has to lie with the federal government and in its executive: the leadership comes from the presidency.

As the opposition of states' rights and civil rights in this illustration suggests, the claim of the states to be free of interference is an issue of liberty also. And at this point the matter becomes very complicated indeed. Whose liberty is to be protected? If the federal government intervenes in Mississippi, isn't there an infringement of freedom? This question inevitably becomes entangled with questions on the meaning of self-government. If the states are taken as hard, concrete entities, the significant conclusion is that federal intervention on behalf of Negroes is interference with the freedom of the states. If the states are not regarded as such concrete entities, however, the conclusion is very different. The conflict then appears as between different sets of human individuals. It is in this latter light that the presidency must be seen as a defender of freedom. Quite understandably, those groups which have benefited from local systems of unequally distributed power will not so regard it.

The Fragmented Authority

A strong tradition of mistrust for the presidency has always existed and it has always been related to fear of tyranny. This mistrust, in some respects a very healthy one, is a compound of rather different fears. One of these has been essentially a fear of loss of state autonomy to a supposedly grasping central authority. This, in turn, is related to the less publicized but probably more keenly felt fear that expanded presidential power might undermine the systems of power of interest group elites that have thrived on a pattern of government decentralization. The most lurid fear, however, is that the President might gather all the threads of power into his hands and establish himself as a dictator. From the early days of the republic down to the time of Andrew Jackson this was expressed as fear of a re-established monarchy. Except for the language, however, essentially the same charges have been directed against Lyndon Johnson. Just what is the justification for this persistent fear?

The strongest part of any justification lies in the President's powers in military and foreign affairs. It was on this that the French critic Riencourt based his alarming picture of the coming Caesars, the Caesars in question being future American Presidents. In an immediate, and genuinely alarming, sense, the powers of the President in time of war are great. As commander-in-chief he can act with seemingly few limitations. That during the last wars in which the United States has engaged the infringements upon liberty made in the President's name have been relatively moderate in no way mitigates the danger that exists. The vagueness of the constitutional authority of the President suggests that the possibilities of presidential action in crisis may not yet have been fully exploited. And it is worth recalling that some of the actions which have been taken have been very strong indeed. The shameful and arbitrary invasions of the rights of Japanese-Americans in World War II should not be forgotten.

It is doubtful, however, whether the threats to liberty in war that may be made by the President or in his name are possible simply because presidential authority is vaguely defined in the Constitution. Probably the most serious invasions of individual rights by presidential action came from Lincoln. Some of these actions were indeed found to be beyond his constitutional powers, but only after the crisis had passed. Supreme Court review of the dubious questions related to the Japanese-American evacuation also took years. The unfortunate fact seems to be that during wartime crises constitutional limitations are brushed aside, and little recourse for the injured is possible so long as the crisis lasts. Moreover, it is also doubtful whether the fact that presidential authority is sometimes the ground cited for arbitrary actions is important. Given a sufficient crisis—and war is almost invariably sufficient—Congress is usually willing to pass measures giving a color of legality to almost anything the President and his military advisers urge as necessary. There is little evidence to justify a belief that Congress is a better guardian of individual liberties in wartime than the President, or that any formally stated constitutional provisions could prevent future outrages of the sort we have already seen. The principle at work here seems to be *inter arma silent leges*.

The really awesome, and frightening, fact about the modern presidency is that while the office has increasingly become the primary medium for responsible government in the United States, the President does not control government in either making or administering policy. It is difficult to foresee that any President ever will have such control. The United States is too large, too diverse, and given to too rapid change for firm control from the White House ever to be possible. Moreover, the remarkable system of devolution of the work of government to separate systems of governance in each of which interest groups, local elites, congressmen, and other public representatives assume autonomous control over a particular area of public policy is so strongly established that nothing is likely to produce any radical change in American ways of government in a short time.

The resulting fragmentation of American policy has nevertheless conferred real benefits on the nation. The primary benefit is that power-holding groups have been induced by their cooptation into these many sub-systems of government to acquiesce in the continuation of the

United States as a nation and have concurrently been made willing to accept a minimum number of national objectives and national policies. By leaving many public policies to be carried out by the states, localities, and even by private associations, whether through grants-in-aid, schemes of "consultation," or the creation of autonomous administrative bodies, stability has been achieved where a more rigid and a more centralized system might long ago have broken apart. Every man who has reached the Presidency has had at least an intuitive appreciation of these benefits.

In accepting the power and the participation of these many political sub-systems, however, a President accepts strong limitations upon his own power—and upon the obligations he has to those of his constituents not fortunate enough to be included within any of the sub-systems which are coopted. Each time the President "consults" with a major farm organization in his choice of a secretary of Agriculture, each time he chooses a major corporation executive to head the Department of Defense or a leading banker for secretary of the Treasury, he yields up a significant part of his ability to affect the policies controlled by those departments. In these and many other ways, he concedes that he must have the support of power-holding elements in the nation. And he has little other choice than to act in this manner. At best, he may cut to a minimum the concessions he is obliged to make.

By thus insuring at least a minimum of national unity and domestic peace, however, a President repudiates a substantial part of the obligation under which he was elected. This cruel dilemma is almost never explicitly acknowledged. The folklore of American politics, with its glorification of decentralization and deep fear of dictatorship and of government in general, makes possible the presentation of the concessions as themselves a form of democracy. The deference to power-holding groups thus appears as democratic self-determination and the avoidance of compulsion (which is conveniently left to the autonomous sub-systems themselves).

The President, nonetheless, remains in office as the elected representative of *all* the people. He must speak and act for those individuals outside the effective schemes of representation and power built upon the fragmented pattern of representation in Congress and the states. He must also see the demands of the many elements of the population in relation to each other and to the needs of the nation as a whole, and if he does not take a view that includes the powerless as well as the powerful, the national interest as well as the particular interests, there is nobody else who can.

In the past the nation was much larger in relation to its population than now; with poor communications the nation could realistically be regarded as a collection of separate parts. The economy was much less integrated, and America's place in the world allowed it the luxury of safe isolation. Inevitably, modern conditions have vastly expanded the obligations of the presidency. Foreign policy cannot be left to the play of contending domestic factions without serious danger. The educational needs of the nation cannot be simply declared a matter for localities to pay for or to decide. Natural resources cannot be given over to exploitive interests to do with as they will. So it is in many areas. The federal government again and again is compelled, by the rising demands from hitherto powerless groups and by dangers visible from a national perspective, to take new kinds of action. The federal government, however, is still highly fragmented and subject to the power of elites of various kinds. Thus, here again, the needs can only be met if the responsibility is accepted in the White House.

If the responsibility of the presidency is large and growing, the power of the office is often inadequate. One of the greatest dangers to American democracy is that the gap between the power and the responsibility of the presidency may widen. To the degree that the two are disproportionate, the nation will be in danger from foreign threats and domestic disorder. To the degree that the President is unable to meet his obligations, demands for justice by deprived minorities will go unsatisfied and the quality of life in many ways will be poorer than it might be. The obligation of the President in the largest terms is to mobilize political power and to direct it toward the ends of social justice and national security. But in the existing American context presidential power is limited.

For this reason, any President has to be concerned continually with the capacities of his own office. He is endowed at election with the aura that goes to the chief of state of the most powerful nation of the world. He receives adulation on a scale known to few other men. He bears the powers acknowledged as his under the Constitution and many legislative acts. He is head of the armed forces and the entire executive branch. He is head of his party. And yet the power that he can assume from these sources is often insufficient and indeed sometimes illusory. Like a general, he has continually to choose among the possible battles he might join, avoiding some and engaging in others. He must build his power for the contests he cannot avoid.

The presidency is not and never can be a machine that runs itself or continues in operation untended. Though the vastly increased demands upon the office have brought about a substantial increase in the Executive Office, routinization of the presidency has not been achieved. This is not because the work load of the office, great though it is, is too vast to be encompassed by competent organization. It has been suggested that the load upon the President is so crushing it should be divided among a number of men, assistant presidents, or a cabinet of vice presidents. While undoubtedly some presidential chores could be well done by assistants, most of the work of the presidency cannot be divided or given over to others, whatever their title, without a radical and probably dangerous change in the system of responsibility. If the assistant presidents were chosen by the President himself and received their commission directly from him, the situation would hardly be different from the present, in which a sufficient number of assistants is available to the President. If, on the other hand, the assistant presidents were to be chosen by election or by Congress—or by any method which gave them authority in any degree independent of the President—the way would be open to a further division of responsibility in an already too fragmented political system. The President's burden may be crushing, but he must carry it.

Without question, there are genuine dangers in our dependence on this office and on a single man. While some of these dangers consist of the possibility that a President may abuse his power, the most serious are that a President will not use his power wisely, or not use it at all when it is needed. For better or worse, a President must be a leader— and a national leader. His power will depend less on the terms of the Constitution or of legislation than on how much he is able to articulate the aspirations of the American people and apply them to national problems. This may involve him at one moment in bitter struggle for the passage of some reform or even in leading the conduct of a great war. But at another moment it may require his bearing of great sorrow, as Lincoln at Gettysburg. Ultimately, like Lincoln, he must become the medium of national reconciliation and rededicate the nation toward its own best ends.

The Presidents

George Washington	1789–1797
John Adams	1797–1801
Thomas Jefferson	1801–1809
James Madison	1809–1817
James Monroe	1817–1825
John Quincy Adams	1825–1829
Andrew Jackson	1829–1837
Martin Van Buren	1837–1841
William Henry Harrison	1841
John Tyler	1841–1845
James K. Polk	1845–1849
Zachary Taylor	1849–1850
Millard Fillmore	1850–1853
Franklin Pierce	1853–1857
James Buchanan	1857–1861
Abraham Lincoln	1861–1865
Andrew Johnson	1865–1869
Ulysses S. Grant	1869–1877
Rutherford B. Hayes	1877–1881
James A. Garfield	1881
Chester A. Arthur	1881–1885
Grover Cleveland	1885–1889
Benjamin Harrison	1889–1893
Grover Cleveland	1893–1897
William McKinley	1897–1901
Theodore Roosevelt	1901–1909
William Howard Taft	1909–1913
Woodrow Wilson	1913–1921
Warren G. Harding	1921–1923
Calvin Coolidge	1923–1929
Herbert Hoover	1929–1933
Franklin Delano Roosevelt	1933–1945

Harry S. Truman	1945–1953
Dwight D. Eisenhower	1953–1961
John F. Kennedy	1961–1963
Lyndon B. Johnson	1963–

THE CONSTITUTION ON THE PRESIDENCY

ARTICLE II

SECTION 1. 1. The executive power shall be vested in a President of the United States of America. He shall hold his office during the term of four years, and, together with the Vice-President, chosen for the same term, be elected as follows:

2. Each state shall appoint, in such manner as the legislature thereof may direct, a number of electors, equal to the whole number of Senators and Representatives to which the State may be entitled in the Congress; but no Senator or Representative, or person holding an office of trust or profit under the United States, shall be appointed an elector.

3.* The electors shall meet in their respective states and vote by ballot for two persons, of whom one at least shall not be an inhabitant of the same state with themselves. And they shall make a list of all the persons voted for, and of the number of votes for each; which list they shall sign and certify, and transmit sealed to the seat of the government of the United States, directed to the President of the Senate. The President of the Senate shall, in the presence of the Senate and House of Representatives, open all the certificates, and the votes shall then be counted. The person having the greatest number of votes shall be the President, if such a number a majority of the whole number of electors appointed; and if there be more than one who have such majority, and have an equal number of votes, then the House of Representatives shall immediately choose by ballot one of them for President; and if no person have a majority, then from the five highest on the list the said House shall in like manner choose the President. But in choosing the President the votes shall be taken by states, the representation from each state having one vote; a quorum for this purpose shall consist of a member or members from two-thirds of the states, and a majority of all the states shall be necessary to a choice. In every case, after the choice of the President, the person having the greatest number of votes of the electors shall be the Vice-President. But if there should remain two or more who have equal votes, the Senate shall choose from them by ballot the Vice-President.

4. The Congress may determine the time of choosing the electors and the day on which they shall give their votes, which day shall be the same throughout the United States.

5. No person except a natural born citizen, or a citizen of the United States, at the time of the adoption of this Constitution, shall be eligible to the office of President; neither shall any person be eligible to that office who shall not have

---

* This paragraph was superseded by the Twelfth Amendment.

attained to the age of thirty-five years, and been fourteen years a resident within the United States.

6. In case of the removal of the President from office, or of his death, resignation, or inability to discharge the powers and duties of the said office, the same shall devolve on the Vice-President, and the Congress may by law provide for the case of removal, death, resignation, or inability, both of the President and Vice-President, declaring what officer shall then act as President, and such officer shall act accordingly until the disability be removed or a President shall be elected.

7. The President shall, at stated times, receive for his services a compensation, which shall neither be increased nor diminished during the period for which he shall have been elected, and he shall not receive within that period any other emolument from the United States or any of them.

8. Before he enter on the execution of his office he shall take the following oath or affirmation:

I do solemnly swear (or affirm) that I will faithfully execute the office of President of the United States, and will to the best of my ability preserve, protect, and defend the Constitution of the United States.

SECTION 2. 1. The President shall be Commander-in-Chief of the Army and Navy of the United States, and of the militia of the several states when called into the actual service of the United States; he may require the opinion, in writing, of the principal officer in each of the executive departments, upon any subject relating to the duties of their respective offices, and he shall have power to grant reprieves and pardons for offenses against the United States, except in cases of impeachment.

2. He shall have power, by and with the advice and consent of the Senate, to make treaties, provided two-thirds of the Senators present concur; and he shall nominate, and, by and with the advice and consent of the Senate, shall appoint ambassadors, other public ministers and consuls, judges of the Supreme Court, and all other officers of the United States, whose appointments are not herein otherwise provided for, and which shall be established by law; but the Congress may by law vest the appointment of such inferior officers, as they think proper, in the President alone, in the courts of law, or in the heads of departments.

3. The President shall have power to fill up all vacancies that may happen during the recess of the Senate, by granting commissions which shall expire at the end of their next session.

SECTION 3. He shall from time to time give to the Congress information of the state of the union, and recommend to their consideration such measures as he shall judge necessary and expedient; he may, on extraordinary occasions, convene both houses, or either of them, and in case of disagreement between them with respect to the time of adjournment, he may adjourn them to such time as he shall think proper; he shall receive ambassadors and other public ministers; he shall take care that the laws be faithfully executed, and shall commission all the officers of the United States.

SECTION 4. The President, Vice-President, and all civil officers of the United States shall be removed from office on impeachment for and conviction of treason, bribery, or other high crimes and misdemeanors.

OTHER PROVISIONS

ARTICLE I

SECTION 3. 6. The Senate shall have the sole power to try all impeachments. When sitting for that purpose, they shall be on oath or affirmation. When the President of the United States is tried, the Chief Justice shall preside; and no person shall be convicted without the concurrence of two-thirds of the members present.

SECTION 7. 2. Every bill which shall have passed the House of Representatives and the Senate shall, before it becomes a law, be presented to the President of the United States; if he approve he shall sign it, but if not he shall return it, with his objections to that house in which it shall have originated, who shall enter the objections at large on their journal and proceed to reconsider it. If after such reconsideration two-thirds of that house shall agree to pass the bill, it shall be sent, together with the objections, to the other house, by which it shall likewise be reconsidered, and if approved by two-thirds of that house it shall become a law. But in all such cases the votes of both houses shall be determined by yeas and nays, the names of the persons voting for and against the bill shall be entered on the journal of each house respectively. If any bill shall not be returned by the President within ten days (Sundays excepted) after it shall have been presented to him, the same shall be a law, in like manner as if he had signed it unless the Congress by their adjournment prevent its return, in which case it shall not be a law.

3. Every order, resolution, or vote to which the concurrence of the Senate and House of Representatives may be necessary (except on a question of adjournment) shall be presented to the President of the United States; and before the same shall take effect, shall be approved by him, or being disapproved by him, shall be repassed by two-thirds of the Senate and House of Representatives, according to the rules and limitations prescribed in the case of a bill.

AMENDMENT XII

The electors shall meet in their respective states and vote by ballot for President and Vice-President, one of whom, at least, shall not be an inhabitant of the same state with themselves; they shall name in their ballots the person voted for as President, and in distinct ballots the person voted for as Vice-President, and they shall make distinct lists of all persons voted for as President and of all persons voted for as Vice-President, and of the number of votes for each; which lists they shall sign and certify, and transmit sealed to the seat of the government of the United States, directed to the President of the Senate. The President of the Senate shall, in the presence of the Senate and House of Representatives, open all the certificates and the votes shall then be counted. The person having the greatest number of votes for President shall be the President, if such number be a majority of the whole number of electors appointed; and if no person have such majority, then from the persons having the highest numbers not exceeding three on the list of those voted for as President, the House of Representatives shall choose immediately, by ballot, the President. But in choosing the President the votes shall be taken by states, the representation from each state having one vote; a quorum for this purpose shall consist of a member or members from two-thirds of the states, and a majority of all the states shall be necessary to a choice. And if the House of Representatives shall not choose a President whenever the right of choice shall devolve upon them, before the fourth day of March next following, then the Vice-President shall act as President, as in the case of the death or other constitutional disability of the President.

The person having the greatest number of votes as Vice-President shall be the Vice-President, if such number be a majority of the whole number of electors appointed; and if no person have a majority, then from the two highest numbers on the list the Senate shall choose the Vice-President; a quorum for the purpose shall consist of two-thirds of the whole number of Senators, and a majority of the whole number shall be necessary to a choice. But no person constitutionally ineligible to the office of President shall be eligible to that of Vice-President of the United States.

AMENDMENT XX

SECTION 1. The terms of the President and Vice-President shall end at noon on the 20th day of January, and the terms of Senators and Representatives at noon on the 3d day of January, of the years in which such terms would have ended if this article had not been ratified; and the terms of their successors shall then begin.

SECTION 2. The Congress shall assemble at least once in every year, and such meeting shall begin at noon on the 3d day of January, unless they shall by law appoint a different day.

SECTION 3. If, at the time fixed for the beginning of the term of the President, the President elect shall have died, the Vice-President elect shall become President. If a President shall not have been chosen before the time fixed for the beginning of his term, or if the President elect shall have failed to qualify, then the Vice-President elect shall act as President until a President shall have qualified; and the Congress may by law provide for the case wherein neither a President elect nor a Vice-President elect shall have qualified, declaring who shall then act as President, or the manner in which one who is to act shall be selected, and such person shall act accordingly until a President or Vice-President shall have qualified.

SECTION 4. The Congress may by law provide for the case of the death of any of the persons from whom the House of Representatives may choose a President whenever the right of choice shall have devolved upon them, and for the case of the death of any of the persons from whom the Senate may choose a Vice-President whenever the right of choice shall have devolved upon them.

AMENDMENT XXII

No person shall be elected to the office of the President more than twice, and no person who has held the office of President, or acted as President, for more

mission produced one of the best studies of contemporary federalism in its *Report* (The Commission on Intergovernmental Relations, 1955). Walter Lippmann's despair of rational public participation in matters relating to foreign affairs is expressed in his *Essays in the Public Philosophy* (Boston: Little, Brown, 1955). A suggestion for change in the presidential system has been made by Herman Finer in *The Presidency: Crisis and Regeneration* (Chicago: The University of Chicago, 1960).

Adams, Sherman, 50, 60
Administrative talent, 83
Agricultural Extension Service, 68
Alien and Sedition Acts, 88
Ambassadors, 73
American Farm Bureau Federation, 68
American people, presidency and, 7, 15, 35
  and presidential campaigns, 17-18
  represented by President, 35, 51, 74, 94
Appropriations, curtailment of, 50
Arkansas, 84, 91
Articles of Confederation, 3, 89-90

Bay of Pigs, 2, 58
  (*See also* Cuba)
Bills, 47
  sponsored by President, 48-49
Binkley, Wilfred, 37
Blough, Roger, 81
Britain, 37, 45-46, 90
Brownlow Committee, 60, 65
Bryce, Lord, quoted, 10
Buchanan, James, 36

Budget, 41-43
  (*See also* Bureau of the Budget)
Budget and Accounting Act, 41
Budget Message, 43
Bundy, McGeorge, 61
Bureau of the Budget, 41-43, 60, 62-68
  size of, 63
Bureaucracy, 53, 55-56
  responsibility of, 56-58
Burns, James M., 45
Burr, Aaron, 19
Business Advisory Council, 81

Cabinet, the, 59-60
  (*See also* Department Secretaries)
Campaigning, 16-17, 28-32
Candidates, congressional, 46
  presidential (*see* Presidential candidates)
Checks and balances, 14, 34
Civil rights, 88, 92
Civil servants, 55, 58
Civil service, 53, 57
Civil War, 10, 18, 36

Commander-in-chief, President as, 5-6, 10, 93
Committees, congressional, 48, 74
Communications, 39-40, 96
  (*See also* Radio; Television)
Congress, 3-7, 88-89
  and the budget, 41
  committees in, 48, 74
  Eightieth, 38
  and foreign policy, 49-50
  and individual liberties, 94
  messages to, 43
  party organization in, 43-46
  powers of, 6, 9, 79
  President and, 6, 8-11, 13-14, 19, 34-51, 74
  as representative of states, 35, 47, 51, 91
  special interests and groups in, 46-48
  (*See also* House of Representatives; Senate)
Congressional Government, Wilson, 11
Congressional investigations, 50
Congressmen, 35, 44, 46, 50, 75, 91
  election of, 38, 51
  and lobbying, 47
  and logrolling, 48, 92
Constituencies, congressional, 35, 47, 51, 92
  presidential, 74
  Supreme Court, 91
Constitution, the, 9, 14, 36, 41, 47, 53, 59, 69, 79, 86-89, 94, 96-97
  First Amendment, 47
  Fourteenth Amendment, 90
  framers of, 2, 5, 8, 19, 34, 50, 87, 89
  quoted, 4, 52
Constitutional powers, 3-7, 53, 59, 69, 79, 96-97
Coolidge, Calvin, quoted, 51
Corwin, Edward S., 8
  quoted, 39
Council of Economic Advisors, 63-66
Courts, 53
  (*See also* Supreme Court)
Crises, 81
Cuba, 2, 78, 81
  (*See also* Bay of Pigs)
Culture, 84

Decision-making, 77-81
Declaration of Independence, 3

Democracy, campaigning and, 17-18
  danger to, 96
  presidential elections and, 33
Democrats, 26, 30-31, 37-38, 42, 45-46, 57
Department of Agriculture, 66-67
Department of Commerce, 66, 81
Department of the Interior, 66-67
Department Secretaries, 66, 95
Depressions, 65
  (*See also* Great Depression)
Dien Bien Phu, 80
Diplomacy, 80
Dirksen, Everett M., 46

Economic Report, 43
Economy, the, 64, 95
Eisenhower, Dwight D., 13-14, 23, 31-32, 39, 42, 46, 50, 57, 64, 72-73, 75-76, 79-80, 84, 91
Eisenhower administration, 61-62
Elections, congressional, 38
  local, 22
  presidential (*see* Presidential elections)
Electoral ballots, 19
Electoral college, 19
Electorate, appeal to, 50
  responsibility to, 55-56
  (*See also* Voters)
Employment Act of 1946, 43, 63-64
Executive branch, 51-68
Executive departments, 5-6
Executive machinery, 53-56
Executive Mansion and Grounds, 60
Executive Office, 58-62, 97
Experts, 58

Factions, 47
Farm Security Administration, 68
Farmers, 32
Federal agencies, autonomy of, 65-68
  rivalry among, 75
Federal government, fragmentation of, 96
  number of employees in, 56
Federal Reserve Board, 40, 66
Federalism, 4, 19, 87-93
Federalist, The, 5
Fiscal (tax) policy, 40
Ford, Henry Jones, quoted, 3

Foreign affairs, 12, 40, 79-80, 93
  public opinion and, 80
Foreign policy, 49, 96
Forest Service, 67

Garner, John Nance, 28
Goldwater, Barry, 26, 31, 45
Government, balanced, 5
  congressional, 37, 44-45
  federal (see Federal government)
  intricate concerns of, 39-40
  modern, character of, 77
  popular, 35
  responsible, 54-55
  sub-systems of, 94-95
Governors, 23
Great Depression, 32 37-38
Groups, 46-48
  presidential decisions and, 54-55

Hamilton, Alexander, 5, 7-8
Harding, Warren G., 1, 23
Hodges, Luther, 81
Hoover, Herbert, 12, 38, 83
Hoover Commissions, 67
Hopkins, Harry L., 61-62
House, Colonel E. M., 61
House of Representatives, 8, 20, 36
  (See also Congress)

Impeachment, 5, 36
In re Neagle, 53
Intelligence, 84

Jackson, Andrew, 8-9, 13, 36, 93
Japanese-Americans, 94
Jefferson, Thomas, 8, 19, 36
Johnson, Lyndon B., 3, 13-14, 28, 38,
  42, 45-46, 49, 58, 64, 66, 74-76,
  80, 93

Kefauver, Estes, 24
Kennedy, John Fitzgerald, 1-3, 13, 19,
  24, 26, 38, 46, 58-59, 62, 64, 70-72,
  74-76, 78, 80-81, 84
Kennedy administration, 60
Keynes, John Maynard, 43, 64
Keynesian economics, 40
Khrushchev, 2, 81
Korean War, 31, 79

Labor, management and, 75

Laski, Harold, quoted, 14
Law-making, President and, 39
  (See also Legislation)
Laws, execution of, 5-6, 53
Leaders, national, 79
  natural, 82
  political, 78
Leadership, 10, 13, 32
  party, 36
  passive, 14
  presidential, 68-85
League of Nations, 12, 37, 49, 76
Legislation, 73, 77
  national scope of, 39-40
  presidential, 39-43
  tariff, 47
Liberty, 92, 94
Lincoln, Abraham, 1, 10, 13, 32, 36-37,
  94, 97
Lippmann, Walter, 80
  quoted, 76
Little Rock, 84, 91
Lobbyists, 47
Logrolling, 48, 92

MacArthur, General, 13
McCarthy, Senator, 39, 72
McKinley, William, 8
Madison, James, 8, 47, 89
Management, labor and, 75
Marshall, John, 8
Marshall Plan, 13
Martin, William M., 66
Military affairs, 93
Minorities, 90
Mississippi, 92
Mobilization, 62
Monetary policy, 40
Monroe, James, 8

National conventions, 23-28
  delegates to, 24-26
  oratory at, 27
National Security Council, 62-63
National unity, 95
Negroes, 30, 92-93
  (See also Civil rights)
Neustadt, Richard, 42
Neutrality, 7-8
New Deal, 30, 38, 45, 60, 67, 91
Nixon, Richard M., 30
North Vietnam, 80

Oath of office, 5-6
Office of Emergency Planning, 60, 62
Office of Science and Technology, 62
Officers, commissioning of, 5-6

Pardons, power to give, 5-6
Party discipline, 45
Party organization, legislative, 43-46
Party system, 44, 46
Patronage, 50, 58
Peace, domestic, 94
  government during, 4
People's choice, presidency and, 16-33
Platforms, 21
Policy, fragmentation of, 94-95
  (*See also* kind of policy, as Foreign
  policy)
Political appointees, 57-58
Political conventions (*see* National con-
  ventions)
Political order, presidency and, 86-97
Political parties, 20, 26, 30-33
  function of, 21
  local, 22-23
  organization of, 22, 46
  use of, 20-24
  (*See also* Democrats; Republicans;
  entries under Party)
Political system, American, 4, 18
  (*See also* Democracy; Government)
Politics, 21, 95
  elections and, 17-18
  federal agencies and, 65
Populists, 32
Power, of Congress, 6, 36
  constitutional (*see* Constitutional
  powers)
  executive, 53
  to govern, 19
  nuclear, 2
  organized, 92
  political, 75
  of presidency, 2-3, 5-9, 11, 13-15, 36,
  69-71, 73-74, 79
  of states, 4
  veto, 50, 77-78
Presidency, the, character of, 1-2
  concepts of, 7-8
  Congress and, 7, 34-51
  federalism and, 87-93
  formulation of, 4-7
  fragmented authority of, 93-97

Presidency (*continued*)
  limitations of, 10
  mistrust of, 93
  myth and symbol of, 1-15
  and people's choice, 16-23
  in the political order, 86-97
  power of, 2-3, 5-9, 11, 13-15, 36, 69-
  71, 73-74, 79
  President's influence on, 2, 7
  requirements for, 19
  responsiblity of, 96
  role of, 55
  routinization of, 97
  Supreme Court and, 7
President, the, authority of, 7, 12-13
  fragmented, 93-97
  and capacity for action, 9
  character and personality of, 38, 73,
  76, 82-85
  as Chief Executive, 52-68, 90
  and Congress, 6, 8-11, 13-14, 19, 34-
  51, 74
  death of, 1
  and decision-making, 77-81
  and the electorate, 55
  eligibility and choice of, 5
  functions and duties of, 5-6, 11-12, 73
  and law-making, 39-43
  as leader, 68-85
  measuring success of, 48-51
  messages to Congress by, 43
  mobilizing support for, 74-76
  popularity of, 9, 74
  power of, 2, 5-15, 53, 69-71, 73-74,
  79, 83-84, 97
  limitation of, 14-15, 95-96
  and the presidency, 2, 7
  prestige of, 70-73
  qualifications for, 23
  re-election of, 29-30
  as representative of the people, 35,
  51, 74, 94
  style of, 3, 75
  work of, 7-14
Presidential appointments, 50
Presidential assistants, 47, 50, 59, 61
Presidential candidates, 23-24, 26
  campaigning by, 16-17, 28-32
Presidential elections, 17-33
  constitutional provision for, 19-20
  importance of, 22
Press conferences, 73

Prestige, presidential, 70-73
Primaries, 24-28
Progressivism, 24
Public opinion, foreign affairs and, 80, 83

Racial segregation, 90-91
Radio, 12-13, 50
Report of the Economic Advisors, 43
Republicans, 26, 30-31, 38-39, 42, 46, 84
Responsibility, bureaucratic, 56-58
    of government, 54
    of presidency, 96
Revolutionary War, 3-4
Riencourt, Amaury de, 93
    quoted, 2
Rights, civil, 88, 92
    individual, 94
    states' (see States' rights)
Rivers and Harbors bills, 48
Roosevelt, Franklin D., 1-2, 12-13, 38, 45, 50, 61, 67-68, 74, 83, 91
Roosevelt, Theodore, 3, 11, 37, 69-70
    quoted, 11
Russia (see Soviet Union)

Secret Service, 70
Senate, the, 5-6, 44, 49-50, 79
    (See also Congress)
Senators, 23, 35, 44, 46, 50, 75, 91
Separation of powers, 4-6, 34-35, 37, 87
South, the, 30
South Vietnam, 80
Southeast Asia, 80
Soviet Union, 2, 78
Special interests, 46-48
Specialists, 58-59
Speeches, President's, 73
State Department, 61
State legislatures, 19
State of the Union message, 5-6, 43
States, Congress as representative of, 35, 91
    freedom of, 92-93
    power of, 4
States' rights, 9, 88, 92-93
Steel, crisis of 1952, 71-72, 78, 81

Stevens, Secretary of the Army, 72
Strikes, 53
Supreme Court, 5, 7, 38, 53, 77, 86 90-91, 94

Taft, William Howard, 3
    quoted, 11-12
Taft-Hartley Act, 78
Tariffs, 47
Television, 26, 50, 74
Tonkin, Gulf of, 80
Treaty making, 5-6
Truman, Harry S., 2, 13, 38, 42, 53, 64, 70, 78, 80
Two-party system, 20, 30, 32

U.S. Public Health Service, 68
United States Steel Corporation, 71-72, 81, 84

Vermont, 30
Veto power, 50, 77-78
Vice President, 4-5, 19
    as assistant to President, 59
    nomination of, 27-28
Vietnam, 58, 79-80
Voters, 17-18
    (See also Electorate)
Votes, electoral, 19-20
    Negro, 30
    popular, 20

Wage Stabilization Board, 78
War, liberty and, 94
    modern, 10
    (See also name of war, as World War II)
War power, 10, 12, 37, 79, 93
Washington, George, 2, 7-8
White House, 60-62, 70-71
White House staff, 62
Willkie, Wendell, 23
Wilson, Woodrow, 11-12, 37, 47-49, 61, 75-76
    quoted, 2, 36
World War II, 41, 45, 94

Youngstown, decision of 1952, 53, 91

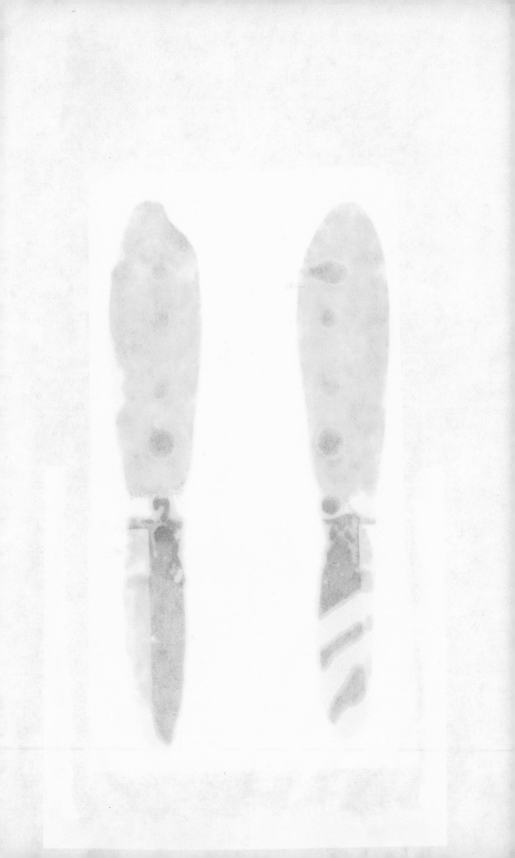

DATE DUE